End-Time Hope

A Journey to Eternity

Mark A. Finley

Pacific Press® Publishing Association
Nampa, Idaho
Oshawa, Ontario, Canada

Cover design by Steve Lanto
Cover design resources from dreamstime.com
Inside design by Kristin Hansen-Mellish

Copyright © 2012 by Pacific Press® Publishing Association
Printed in the United States of America
All rights reserved

You can obtain additional copies of this book by calling toll-free 1-800-765-6955 or by visiting http://www.adventistbookcenter.com.

Library of Congress Cataloging-in-Publication Data:

Finley, Mark, 1945-
  End time hope : a journey to eternity / Mark A. Finley.
    p. cm.
  ISBN 13: 978-0-8163-3791-0 (pbk.)
  ISBN 10: 0-8163-3791-8 (pbk.)
  1. Second Advent. 2. End of the world. 3. Bible—Prophecies.
I. Title.

  BT886.3.F55 2012
  236'.9—dc23

                                                          2012025147

12 13 14 15 16 • 5 4 3 2 1

Contents

With Special Thanks

Most books are not the product of only one person's thoughts. Nor are they produced by hours of research alone. They are much more. They are the result of years of life experience. For forty-five years, I have had the privilege of preaching on the hope of the Second Advent to audiences in more than eighty countries on almost every continent in the world. I never tire of seeing the sparkle in people's eyes and the joy on their faces as they grasp the incredible good news that Jesus is really coming again. Daily I am reminded of the great privilege I have had for decades of sharing this hope with hundreds of thousands of people both in person and through the mass media. I thank God for this awesome privilege.

I would also like to express special thanks to Steve Mosley, our script writer at *It Is Written* television. During the past twelve years, Steve and I have collaborated on a number of projects, and many of the thoughts in this volume appeared first in *It Is Written* television scripts. I am indebted to Steve's skillful pen and literary clarity. His contributions have enhanced this work greatly.

I would also like to express my deepest appreciation to my wife, Ernestine. Not only has she encouraged me to write a book on the hope of the Second Coming, but she also has played a significant part in the production of this book. Chapters 2 and 3 are updated expansions of my public evangelistic sermons. She faithfully listened to the audio presentations of these messages and typed them so I could edit the material and prepare it for this manuscript.

I praise God for the privilege of sharing the eternal truths of Scripture, and I hope you will be as blessed reading *End-Time Hope* as I was writing it.

Before You Turn This Page . . .

The United States is more than sixteen trillion dollars in debt, the unemployment rate has gone over 8 percent, and more people are losing their homes than ever before.

College graduates wonder whether they will find a job, retirees are concerned about their retirement accounts, and the international scene is uncertain—is another terrorist attack imminent?

And what's behind all the natural disasters that seem to be ripping town after town apart?

Many people find the time in which we live to be confusing. It seems that twenty-first-century society has lost its moral compass. Long-held moral standards are being cast to the wind, and we're groping around in the dark, looking for the light at the end of the tunnel.

Yet there is hope. That's what this book is about. Every chapter pulsates with hope.

Shortly before Jesus ascended to heaven, He spoke words that brought encouragement to His disciples. He said, "Let not your heart be troubled; you believe in God, believe also in Me. In My Father's house are many mansions; if it were not so, I would have told you. I go to prepare a place for you. And if I go and prepare a place for you, I will come again" (John 14:1–3).

Jesus' promise to return wasn't some make-believe, pious platitude without any substance. It wasn't a warm fuzzy that He gave us merely to make us feel good. His word is sure—a solid foundation for hope in a world that's in deep trouble.

Jesus really is coming again! He really came to this earth once, and He really will come again. But this time He isn't coming as a babe in Bethlehem's manger, but as King of kings and Lord of lords.

One day sickness and sorrow will be perpetually banished.

One day fear and famine will fade into forever.

One day disease, disaster, and death will be gone for good.

One day worry, want, and war will be things of the far-distant past.

One day every tear will be wiped away and every tragedy turned to triumph.

One day our dreams will be fulfilled, and joy will flood our hearts.

One day Jesus will come.

Take a fresh breath of hope as you embark on an incredible journey of discovery through end-time events to eternity.

Chapter 1

The Ultimate Space Journey

On April 17, 2012, the space shuttle *Discovery,* which was bolted on top of a NASA 747 aircraft, soared over the nation's capital in a salute before landing at Washington Dulles International Airport in Washington, D.C. Thousands of people lined the National Mall to catch a glimpse of the famed spacecraft. They applauded wildly as *Discovery* circled the United States Capitol and the Washington Monument and headed for the airport and its final resting place in the Smithsonian Institution.

Aerospace writers described the spectacular scene in these words:

> The world's most traveled spaceship took off at daybreak from Cape Canaveral, Fla., bolted to the top of a modified jumbo jet for the trip.
>
> Three hours later, the pair took a few spins around Washington at an easy-to-spot 1,500-foot altitude before the retired shuttle was grounded for good....
>
> Discovery's list of achievements include delivering the Hubble Space Telescope to orbit, carrying the first Russian cosmonaut to launch on a U.S. spaceship, performing the first rendezvous with the Russian space station Mir with the first female shuttle pilot in the cockpit, returning Mercury astronaut John Glenn to orbit, and bringing shuttle flights back to life after the Challenger and Columbia accidents.[1]

It is difficult to imagine that Discovery traveled a total of 148,221,675 miles on thirty-nine space missions. This is the equivalent of 310 round trips to the moon. What an incredible accomplishment! No wonder so many people wanted one last lingering glance at America's most beloved spacecraft.

There's something fascinating about space travel. It captures our imagination. It stimulates our thinking. It fuels our dreams for a better tomorrow. Maybe—just maybe—there are answers to our deepest questions out there beyond the stars.

The universe is definitely beckoning us. Movie phenomena like the Star Wars series provide just one example of our fascination with space. We want to see what's out there. We want to take the ultimate journey. Some private companies are already advertising trips far out into space and booking seats on rocket ships.

Potentially, people could be rocketed to their space vacations via a commuter space shuttle similar to *Discovery*. A March 24, 2006, Associated Press article on space travel made this intriguing observation:

> If floating weightless and peering down on a shimmering-blue Earth sounds appealing, you might consider being a space tourist. As long as you've got a fat wallet. Two years after the first privately financed space flight jump-started a sleepy industry, more than a dozen companies are developing rocket planes to ferry ordinary rich people out of the atmosphere.[2]

The ultimate space journey

In this chapter, I'll tell you about a space journey that will answer your questions once and for all. It's the ultimate space journey, and it's open to more than just a few astronauts, more than just the elite. It's a journey each of us can take, and it will bring us face-to-face with destiny.

What's more, we don't have to build a warp-speed spaceship in order to make this journey. We'll journey through space. We'll travel beyond the stars, beyond the planets, and through Orion's open space to the heart of the universe.

The apostle Paul was one of many Bible writers who under the inspiration of the Holy Spirit described this ultimate journey. He passed the good news to his fellow believers who worshiped in the church at Thessalonica. Paul wrote,

> If we believe that Jesus died and rose again, even so God will bring with Him those who sleep in Jesus. . . . For the Lord Himself will descend from heaven with a shout, with the voice of an archangel, and with the trumpet of God. And the dead in Christ will rise first. Then we who are alive and remain shall be caught up together with them in the clouds to meet the Lord in the air. And thus we shall always be with the Lord (1 Thessalonians 4:14, 16, 17).

Jesus Christ, the Messiah, the One who paid such a remarkable visit to this planet two thousand years ago, is going to pay us another visit. And He's going to make quite an entrance the next time He comes. He won't be coming as a babe in Bethlehem's manger, but as "KING OF KINGS AND LORD OF LORDS" (Revelation 19:16). And the heavens will rumble with a great shout as trumpets blast and angels sing out.

The Bible refers to this remarkable space journey that brings our Lord to earth again more than fifteen hundred times. Enoch, the seventh from Adam, prophesied that our Lord would return (see Jude 14). David joyfully declared, "Our God shall come, and shall not keep silence" (Psalm 50:3). The angelic beings present at Jesus' ascension encouraged the disciples with these words: "This same Jesus, who was taken up from you into heaven, will so come in like manner as you saw Him go into heaven" (Acts 1:11)

Other texts fill in many more details. Every human eye is going to see this spectacle of an army of angelic beings descending through the sky (Revelation 1:7). The face of the coming Christ will shine like the sun at high noon, and His garments will flash a brilliant white (Revelation 1:12–16).

Jesus and the heavenly host will swoop down in a cloud of glory and circle the earth faster than any spaceship. The ground will shake. Lightning will flash. Mountains will tumble into the sea. Graves will split open, and those who have died in Jesus will rise up from their graves in the cold ground, alive and transformed, now having glorious, immortal bodies. Believers who were alive at Jesus' coming will rise with them right up into the air, drawn to the glorious light of Jesus' presence.

And what happens next? Remember how 1 Thessalonians 4:14 goes? "God will bring with Him . . ." He'll bring believers with Him.

Bring them where?

He'll bring them *from earth to heaven*! He'll raise them from their graves, never to die again, to take a journey to eternity.

Jesus promised us through John: "If I go and prepare a place for you, I will come again and receive you to Myself; that where I am, there you may be also" (John 14:3). That's what is going to happen to all those who've placed their faith in Jesus. We are going to be swept up to heaven in that interstellar cloud. We're going to take a journey so we can always be with the Lord. We're going to take a journey to the place where Jesus has been preparing many mansions. We're going to take a journey to our Father's house.

Friends, this is the ultimate journey. It's the journey to the center of the universe, to the home of God. Talk about discovering where we've come from! Talk about exploring our origins! This formation of angels is going to take us to our Creator. It's going to take us to the place where all our questions will be answered, where our deepest longings will be fulfilled.

Discovering life beyond the stars

NASA's Kepler space telescope is now busy searching for exoplanets—planets in other star system. And 2012 could bring something even more exciting: the first true "alien Earth."

"Just this month, Kepler scientists announced two landmark finds—the first two Earth-size alien planets, as well as a larger world in its star's habitable zone, that just-right range of distances where liquid water (and possibly life as we know it) could exist."[3]

In fact, a whole new science has blossomed around this quest: the science of astrobiology. It uses many different disciplines to try to find life in the universe. Some scientists believe that soon we'll have the technology to search for samples of life on Mars and return those samples to earth safely.

Most scientists don't expect to find a cuddly creature like E.T. anytime soon. They're looking for one-celled organisms that can survive harsh environments. Life is hardier than we used to assume. We've now discovered certain bacteria that can actually survive, and thrive, in glacial ice and in 250-degree heat under the sea.

Human beings are curious about life out there among the stars. We can't help wanting to make contact somehow. Who knows what we might find? Who knows what intelligent beings might start talking back to us?

Well, I have good news about life out there among the stars. We're going to find it. I have good news about signs of intelligence in the universe. Intelligent beings are going to start talking back—in a very big way. We're going to hear the voice of our Creator echoing around our planet. We're going to hear the voices of angelic beings rumbling across the sky like thunder. We're going to have a cosmic rendezvous.

That's the great event that Jesus' disciples tell us is coming. It's more mind-boggling than the Hubble Telescope sighting a new galaxy or scientists discovering some single-celled organism on a distant planet. We're going to come face-to-face with the greatest Intelligence in the universe. His countenance is going to shine down on this world like the sun at high noon.

Yes, Jesus is going to make a very big entrance the second time He comes. Notice this description in Matthew 24:

> As the lightning comes from the east and flashes to the west, so also will the coming of the Son of Man be. . . . The stars will fall from heaven, and the powers of the heavens will be shaken. . . . Then all the tribes of the earth . . . will see the Son of Man coming on the clouds of heaven with power and great glory. And He will send His angels with a great sound of a trumpet, and they will gather together His elect from the four winds, from one end of heaven to the other (Matthew 24:27, 29–31).

The Savior adds this thought-provoking truth: "The Son of Man will come in the glory of His Father with His angels, and then He will reward each according to his works" (Matthew 16:27).

Jesus Christ is going to appear above us, flashing from horizon to horizon. His great angelic spaceship of light will make heaven and earth tremble. And He will gather believers, living and dead, from every corner of the planet. He beckons them to come up to Him. He beckons them to go on a journey.

Oh, yes, signs of intelligent lives in the universe are going to appear. The sign of the Son of God is going to appear. His glory is going to fill the sky.

And all those who have committed their lives to Jesus Christ are going to be able to journey with Him beyond the stars, through the galaxies, to heaven. We'll be traveling with the Son of God, Jesus—in whom are hidden all the treasures of wisdom and knowledge.

You know, when we human beings try to think about *real* space travel, about journeying from one galaxy to the next, the huge distances are overwhelming. How do you reach a star thousands of light-years away? Scientists today can't conceive of traveling faster than the speed of light. So, real space travel faces huge obstacles. But the second coming of Jesus Christ is going to remove all those obstacles. The One who created all these stars and calls them all by name and leads them forth—this God can transport us through the universe as fast as He wants to.

We'll be flying along with Jesus in that angelic formation. Distances won't matter. Black holes won't matter. Even the speed of light won't be a barrier. It is God who beckons us home, and that's all that matters. We'll all arrive safely at our destination, and we'll all arrive together. We'll all stand together on a sea of glass around the throne of God—and sing our hearts out in exultation!

That's the ultimate space journey. And you know, people are becoming increasingly aware that we *need* to take some kind of journey. We need to find something beyond this world.

Why? Because we're using up many natural resources on this planet. Experts have begun to look for new supplies out in space. Some talk of mining asteroids for valuable minerals. In fact, some companies have already started developing plans to mine the moon. The soil on the moon contains very high concentrations of silicon. And there's plenty of iron there too.

This planet is wearing out. It's weighed down with so many problems. People are looking for solutions in outer space. They're thinking and hoping that maybe somehow, somewhere in the vast universe, there's a solution to war and hunger and greed. Maybe we can find a better place.

Our final return

The Bible has more good news for us. Our journey to eternity won't be a one-way trip. It may shock you, but the Bible says that we will make a return journey—to earth. Now there's one end-time event that you may not have heard about before. Of course, we'll make that return trip after we've traveled with Jesus to heaven. It's the last segment of our flight.

Do you remember the statement Jesus made in the Sermon on the Mount about the ultimate fate of God's children? Here it is: "Blessed are the meek, *for they shall inherit the earth*" (Matthew 5:5; emphasis added). David stated this eternal truth in one of the psalms: "The meek shall inherit the earth, and shall delight themselves in the abundance of peace" (Psalm 37:11).

No, the earth that we'll return to won't be like the one we live on today. The Bible says, "We, according to His promise, look for new heavens and a new earth in which righteousness dwells" (2 Peter 3:13).

Earth will be a better place. Sickness, suffering, heartache, and death will be gone forever. Disease and disaster will disappear. Chaos and calamity will be finished. Think of what it will be like to descend from heaven with Jesus, His angels, and all the rest of the heavenly host to a magnificent earth made new in the glory of Eden.

So, we're going to take a second incredible space journey. This time our spaceship will be an entire city—a city that gleams with golden streets and pearly gates. Here's what the apostle John saw in vision:

> I saw a new heaven and a new earth. . . . Then I, John, saw the holy city, New Jerusalem, coming down out of heaven from God, prepared as a bride adorned for her husband. And I heard a loud voice from heaven saying, "Behold, the tabernacle of God is with men, and He will dwell with them" (Revelation 21:1–3).

An entire city is going to appear in the sky! Revelation 20:9 tells us that "the saints"—believers—are inside that "beloved city," the New Jerusalem. They've just made another incredible journey through space. They've come back to the earth. It's now time for "a new heaven and a new earth."

God will burn this world clean of sin and suffering. Then He'll remove the scars. He'll replace the ugliness. He'll re-create the earth.

And then this New Jerusalem will settle down on this planet. It will be our home on earth. And God will live here with us. And from that eternal city we will colonize this renewed planet.

And you know what? The transparent gold of the New Jerusalem's streets won't wear out. Its gates, made of enormous pearls, won't fall off their hinges. The sapphires and emeralds in the city's foundations won't crumble away.

The citizens of the New Jerusalem will be refreshed forever by the river of life that flows through that city. They will be forever renewed by the tree of life in that city, which bears twelve different kinds of fruit.

This is the picture in Revelation. And this picture assures us that we are going to find a forever home of peace and blessing. The life of God will flow from His throne to His people. He, Himself, will be our God. He will light up that city with His everlasting glory. We will live in the warmth of His love and the joy of His presence through the ceaseless ages of eternity.

I want to take that ultimate journey with God. I want to take that great space odyssey. There's got to be more to life than mining minerals on the moon. There's got to be more than poking around on asteroids. There's got to be more than finding renewable energy resources. We need a bigger answer for the longing in our hearts. We need the glory of the Son of righteousness.

The Bible tells us, yes, it's coming. *He's* coming. Jesus is going to make a spectacular appearance the second time He comes.

You'll want to be ready for that event. You'll want to know this Being whose brilliance will flash from horizon to horizon. You'll want to place your faith in the One who will answer back with a voice that thunders across the sky. You'll want to be ready for the ultimate space journey.

It's coming. One day you'll be swept up into the air and into Jesus' arms.

One day you'll journey to heaven in that angelic craft of light.

One day you'll journey back through space in a golden city.

One day you'll live with God on the earth made new.

So be ready.

So look up.

So reach out to the One who is preparing a place for you in His Father's house.

You can decide to commit your life to the living Christ right now. Why not reach out to Him right now by praying this prayer of dedication: "Dear Lord, deep within my heart, I sense that You have plans for me beyond my wildest dreams. Something within me tells me that this world is not all there is. I long to take that eternal space journey with You to my eternal home. I long to see You face to face. Today, I commit my life to You now and forever. In Jesus' name. Amen."

Endnotes

[1] Roz Plater, Brianne Carter, and Jay Korff, "Space shuttle Discovery flies over D.C. landmarks," ABC 7/News Channel 8, April 17, 2012, http://www.wjla.com/articles/2012/04/space-shuttle-discovery-to-fly-over-d-c-landmarks-74857.html.

[2] Associated Press, "Space Travel Price No Longer Out of This World," *Los Angeles Times,* March 24, 2006, http://articles.latimes.com/2006/mar/24/business/fi-spacetour24.

[3] "Why 2012 Could Be the Year We Find a Habitable Planet," *Christian Science Monitor,* http://www.csmonitor.com/Science/2011/1221/Why-2012-could-be-the-year-we-find-a-habitable-planet.

Chapter 2

End-Time Signs

People around the world are perplexed. They wonder what's going to happen next—what's on the horizon. They're concerned about their own futures, and they're concerned about this world's future. The faltering international economy, increased natural disasters, and rising crime and violence have them worried. Unemployment, world hunger, terrorism, and lives that seem meaningless compound their questions about life. This concern is global, affecting people from various backgrounds and cultures.

But the Bible clearly reveals God's plan for the future, and that plan is bright with God's promises! From Genesis to Revelation, the Bible speaks hope to every generation. It reveals Jesus, who came once to redeem us from the penalty and power of sin and who is coming again to deliver us from sin's presence. The last book of the Bible, Revelation, holds out this hope with particular clarity and directness. Its central theme is the return of Jesus. In the first chapter, the author, the apostle John, introduces the return of our Lord with these words: "Behold, He is coming with clouds, and every eye will see Him, even they who pierced Him. And all the tribes of the earth will mourn because of Him. Even so, Amen" (Revelation 1:7).

The book of Revelation goes on to speak with a vibrant urgency about Jesus' return. It lifts our eyes from the earth below to heaven above. It lifts us above the problems, trauma, and disappointments of life to the ultimate solution of earth's problems, of our problems. And, in turn, the last chapter of the book of Revelation radiates with the hope of the second coming of Jesus Christ. Jesus encourages Revelation's readers by repeating His promise three times: "Behold, I am coming quickly!" He says. "Blessed is he who keeps the words of the prophecy of this book" (Revelation 22:7). "Behold, I am coming quickly, and My reward is with Me, to give to every one according to his work" (verse 12). And, "He who testifies to these things says, 'Surely I am coming quickly.' Amen" (verse 20).

The last two verses of the Bible's last chapter conclude with John's earnest prayer: "Even so, come, Lord Jesus! The grace of our Lord Jesus Christ be with you all. Amen" (verses 20, 21).

How quickly is quickly?

The book of Revelation pulsates with the expectation that Jesus is coming soon.

But wait a minute. How soon is soon? How near is near? And how quickly is quickly? Haven't Christians down through the ages believed Jesus was coming soon? Haven't they believed for centuries—for millenniums—that His coming is near?

One evening the famous radio evangelist Pastor H. M. S. Richards of the Voice of Prophecy was preaching to a large audience about the signs of Jesus' coming. A man in the audience, obviously in his seventies, stood up and challenged Pastor Richards's statement that Jesus was coming soon. He said, "Jesus may not come for a hundred years. No one can possibly have any idea when He will come."

Pastor Richards replied, "Sir, judging by your age, it won't be a hundred years for you."

That's true for us too. Jesus' coming is just a heartbeat away for each of us, because when our hearts stop beating, the next thing we'll know is the return of our Lord.

But the question still remains, Is there biblical evidence that Jesus will come soon? Has He left us any signs that indicate how near to the end of the world we are? Did He speak of any events or world conditions that would indicate we are approaching the time of His second coming?

Yes, in a masterful presentation to His disciples recorded in Matthew 24, Jesus did list signs that would mark the end time of this world. He didn't give us an exact date for His return, but He did speak of things that will be present in ever-increasing frequency on an international scale before His return. We will never be told the date of His coming, but we can tell when He is near. Speaking of these signs, Jesus told His disciples, "When you see all these things, know that it is near—at the doors!" (Matthew 24:33). Let's examine Jesus' own list of last-day signs so we, too, may be filled with the hope that His coming is near.

On one occasion, Jesus was sitting on the Mount of Olives with His disciples. From there, they could see the city of Jerusalem spread out before them. Jesus pointed to the magnificent Jewish temple and said, "Not one stone shall be left here upon another, that shall not be thrown down" (verse 2).[1]

The disciples thought that an event as cataclysmic as the destruction of the temple must be the end of the world, so they put the two events together, asking Jesus, "Tell us when will these things be? And what will be the sign of Your coming, and of the end of the age?" (verse 3).

Jesus answered both of their questions. He told them about signs that would precede the destruction of Jerusalem and about signs that would precede His return at the end of the world. Some of the signs of the destruction of Jerusalem were to be repeated before His second coming, though in a larger magnitude and on a worldwide scale. We might say that the signs preceding the destruction of Jerusalem were local signs that will be repeated but on a grander scale—a cosmic scale—just before His return. In this masterful presentation, Jesus summarizes the end-time signs that are to appear in the areas of religion, politics, nature, and society. When we see these signs in the world around us, we know that Jesus' coming is near.

False religious teachers

First, we'll look at signs in the realm of religion. Jesus said that before His return, false or counterfeit religious movements would flourish. He warned, "Many will come in My name . . . and will deceive many" (verse 5). "Then many false prophets will rise up and deceive many" (verse 11). "False christs and false prophets will rise and show great signs and wonders" (verse 24). Notice that Jesus uses the word *many*. There will be *many* false religious teachers and movements, and they will deceive *many*. Before the coming of Christ, we should expect an explosion of interest in false religions, the occult, and psychic phenomena.

During the past decade, the number of people in the United States who identify themselves as belonging to the New Age movement increased by 247 percent. According to the American Religious Identification Survey (ARIS), the number of adults who identify themselves as adherents of the Wiccan, pagan, and spiritualist religions have increased by more than 400 percent in the past two decades. Teens especially are attracted to these occult movements. They outnumber older converts by three to one.

Jesus indicated that we should also expect to see numerous charismatic teachers of religion who make supernatural claims and thus lead people away from the Word of God. He said many of these counterfeit movements will be accompanied by signs and miracles, which some of these false teachers who contradict the Bible will apparently perform.

These times require care in discernment, because counterfeits aren't always easy to detect. We must remember that working what appears to be a miracle doesn't mean that the miracle worker is a servant of God. The Bible teaches that evil spirits can perform miracles too. In fact, Revelation warns of "spirits of demons, performing signs [miracles]" (Revelation 16:14).

To summarize, one of the things we should anticipate before the coming of Jesus is a rise in interest of false teachers—an explosion in the number and popularity of false religious leaders who draw people away from the clear teachings of the Bible. These charlatans will point to the miraculous signs they perform as evidence that what they are teaching is true. But the spirit behind these signs is not the Holy Spirit.

We also see the current popularity of these false religions or substitutes for religion in the fact that the number of books, magazines, movies, TV programs, and Internet sites related to the occult has exploded. People are turning to psychic seers. They're turning to occult artists. A book titled *Angels of Deceit* outlines the many religious deceptions that people are falling for today. These counterfeits are leading men and women away from God's Word. Let me give you a few notable examples.

In March 1997, thirty-eight members of the Heaven's Gate cult joined their leader, Marshall Applewhite, in committing suicide. Why would they do such a thing? They believed that some sort of celestial spacecraft was following the Hale-Bopp comet, which was passing through our region of the solar system at that time, and they were convinced that it would pick them up and miraculously take them to the next level of existence. Applewhite told his followers that planet Earth was about to be recycled, and the only chance to survive was to leave with him. And "to leave" meant to die.

Applewhite deceived his followers with an amazingly distorted view of end-time events. He substituted his word for the Word of God.

But do you know what is even more frightening? When it was discovered that thirty-nine cult members were dead, the authorities put public service announcements on television and radio, saying, "If you don't know where your child is, and you think your child has joined a cult, call us." And over the next few hours, they received fifteen hundred calls from concerned parents who thought their children might be involved in a cult!

Another example

Here is another example. In the 1970s, Jim Jones captured the world's attention. He led 913 members of his religious organization, the Peoples Temple, into deception and ultimately death. But here's the interesting thing: before he led so many people to kill their families and themselves (nearly a thousand died), various government officials had given him support and awards because of his work on behalf of civil rights and racial equality. National and local figures praised him for his community involvement.

But video footage of his church services shows people being pushed down to the altar in wheelchairs and leaving their wheelchairs behind as they ran across the front of the church claiming they were healed. People with cancer claimed their tumors were gone, and multiple other people afflicted with various diseases claimed they were also healed.

These were the people who followed this cult leader to the jungles of Guyana to set up a so-called utopian society, and they ended up committing suicide by drinking Flavor-Aid laced with cyanide. They were deceived and didn't know it. It is a dangerous thing to allow the teachings of any religious leader to substitute for the teachings of the Bible.

The people who accepted David Koresh as their messiah also suffered because of the poor choice they had made. Koresh had some strange teachings about the book of Revelation. He believed he had divine qualities and was the Lamb of Revelation. Koresh believed he could take the wives of the members of his cult as "spiritual wives." Many people who followed him were sincere, but they were sincerely deceived, and they followed him to their deaths. Many of us remember the horror in an FBI agent's voice as he shouted over national television, "Oh my God, they're killing themselves!"

Marshall Applewhite, Jim Jones, and David Koresh are just a few examples of what is happening internationally today. All over the world these types of religious counterfeits and deceivers are arising and leading people to accept their word rather than the plain teachings of the Bible.

According to the Web site www.cultclinic.org, an estimated five to seven million Americans have been involved in cults or cultlike groups, which the clinic estimates number anywhere from three thousand to five thousand. There are approximately 180,000 new recruits to cults every year.[2] The facts confirm that Jesus' warning "Beware of false christs and false prophets" is true. This is certainly a sign of the times.

But Scripture's most urgent warning is about the rise of the most dangerous of all false christs—the antichrist power. The end-time antichrist impersonates Jesus just as do all these other false christs. However, he is so incredibly deceptive that almost all the world ends up following him. Scripture says, "He performs great signs, so that he even makes fire come down from heaven on the earth in the sight of men. And he deceives those who dwell on the earth by those signs which he was granted to do in the sight of the beast" (Revelation 13:13, 14).

The signs Jesus gave in the realm of religion are being fulfilled before our eyes. We will take a more extensive look at the deceptions of the antichrist in a coming chapter.

Political signs

Jesus now moves to the area of politics and world affairs. He foretells the momentous events that will occur on an international scale before His return. He discusses international conflicts and war. Jesus predicts the very events we see occurring around us today.

Throughout the centuries, humankind has always experienced war, but Jesus' predictions go far beyond individual wars. He said that just before His return there won't be just *a* war, but that war will become a way of life for millions. He declared, "You will hear of wars and rumors of wars" (Matthew 24:6).

Someone may ask, Haven't we always had wars down through history? If we've had conflict throughout the centuries, what sense does it make to say war is a sign of the end of the world?

Let's notice carefully what Jesus said. "You will hear of wars and rumors of wars." "Wars" is in the plural. Jesus also predicted that just before the end there will be conflicts on a global scale—in other words, there will be world wars. In fact, Jesus didn't say there would be one war. He said, "Nation will rise against nation, and kingdom against kingdom" (verse 7). What Jesus predicted was not an individual war, but a world engulfed in war.

May I remind you that in the twentieth century, our world experienced World War I and World War II. The twentieth century was the bloodiest century of all time. One sociologist estimated that in that century, war was responsible for the deaths of 231 million people.[3] The world certainly has experienced incredible international conflicts in the past century and in the beginning of this one. In addition to World War I and World War II, America has been involved in the Spanish-American War, the Korean War, the Vietnam War, two wars in Iraq and the war in Afghanistan. There have been other conflicts in which the U.S. was not involved so directly—in the Middle East and in Africa, for instance.

And today there is a new kind of war—terrorism—and our response to that kind of conflict. Terrorists have taken the battle to our streets. Terrorists have struck from Bali to Spain to London to New York City, and there seems to be no end in sight, leaving political leaders wondering where the next terrorist attack will take place.

In recent decades, political leaders have made valiant attempts to attain peace. We certainly applaud their efforts. But we also recognize that we will never have lasting peace until Jesus, the Prince of Peace, comes.

World peace is very fragile. Barely have the signatures on a peace treaty dried when the conflict errupts again. The apostle Paul describes it this way: "When they say, 'Peace and safety!' then sudden destruction comes upon them. . . . And they shall not escape" (1 Thessalonians 5:3).

How many times have you seen television images of Israelis and Arabs expressing a desire for peace in the Middle East? And yet no one can agree on a peace treaty. The conflict flares up again and again. Another terrorist has blown up a bus in Jerusalem. Israel has built more settlements in the occupied territory. Missiles have again been fired from the Gaza Strip.

On the verge of self-destruction

"When they say, 'Peace and safety!' then sudden destruction comes upon them." Centuries-old biblical prophecies are being fulfilled today. For all of its best efforts, the United Nations has failed to achieve world peace. The Bible is accurate. It speaks of our day. Scripture declares Jesus will come at a time when the human race could destroy itself. He'll return to earth at a time when this planet is on the verge of self-destruction. Never before the past century has the human race had that ability. But now, not only are we destroying our environment, but we also have built enough bombs to kill ourselves many times over.

Revelation describes it this way:

> "The nations were angry, and Your wrath has come, and the time of the dead, that they should be judged, and that You should reward Your servants the prophets and the saints, and those who fear Your name, small and great, and should destroy those who destroy the earth" (Revelation 11:18).

When Jesus comes to give out His rewards, He comes also to "destroy those who destroy the earth." Did the human race have the ability to destroy the earth one hundred years ago? Certainly not. But today we do have enough nuclear weaponry to wipe out civilization. Think of the nations that have developed nuclear weaponry: in addition to the United States, Russia, the United Kingdom, France, and China, there now are also India, Pakistan, North Korea, and probably Israel. If Iran doesn't have nuclear capability at this point, it's possible that it soon will.

Are we defusing the nuclear threat? Is the world safer today than it was fifty years ago? *Time* magazine ran an article that reveals that the nuclear threat is not being defused as quickly as we think. Take Russia, for example. After the fall of the Soviet Union, Russia's economy suffered a severe downturn. At a time when Russian scientists and key military personnel were facing pay cuts, the temptation to sell nuclear materials and plans was extremely high. Who knows whether or not all the nuclear materials and plans were kept out of the wrong hands? We do have one example of a nuclear scientist peddling nuclear secrets for financial gain. Pakistan's eminent nuclear scientist Abdul Qadeer Khan sold key nuclear secrets to a number of countries.

The television program *60 Minutes* broadcast an amazing report on Russia's secret nuclear cities. Krasnoyarask, a city of a hundred thousand people in Siberia, was not on any map. Its nuclear reactors produced forty tons of plutonium in forty years. That's enough to make ten thousand nuclear bombs! There were ten of these so-called secret cities in Russia. They were closed off to the public. During the Soviet era, they all produced plutonium, the key element for developing a nuclear bomb. Every three days, each of these cities turned out enough plutonium to make a nuclear bomb. Every three days! In fact, this became such a concern that former U.S. energy secretary Bill Richardson expressed grave concern that terrorists and rogue states have their eyes on Russian plutonium.

A number of years ago, Walter Lippmann, the well-known American newspaper columnist, commented on the threat of a nuclear holocaust. He said, "We are poised on the brink of the most calamitous conflict that can be imagined. Indeed, it cannot even be imagined." And as long ago as 1945, William Ripley of "Believe It or Not" fame expressed his grave fears about the power of the atomic bomb. Reporting from Hiroshima, Japan, the site of the first detonation of an atomic bomb in war, he said, "I am standing on the place where the end of the world began." And here's a sobering thought: never have weapons been invented and then not used.

But this world isn't going to be destroyed in some nuclear holocaust. I think I hear the footsteps of the coming Jesus. I think I hear the drumbeat of the return of our Lord. Time is not some cyclical event that has no terminal point. A conclusion is coming. All history is moving toward a grand climax. The signs of the times indeed are being fulfilled. Jesus has said He will step across the threshold of eternity into time. He will come at a time when the human race has the capacity to destroy itself. He will come to deliver us.

Hope and help are on the way. We can look forward to the coming of Jesus. Although "men's hearts [are] failing them from fear and the expectation of those things which are coming on the earth" (Luke 21:26), we can look forward to a joyous tomorrow.

Jesus says, "Don't look around you; look up. I'll be coming soon!" He invites us to focus on the divine reality that before long He'll be returning to earth. Our world won't be destroyed in some world-engulfing nuclear conflict. It won't end in some cosmic big bang. Despotic world leaders won't have the last word—Jesus will.

The aged apostle John, exiled on the island of Patmos, caught a glimpse of the majesty of Jesus' return. He wrote,

> I saw heaven opened, and behold, a white horse. And He who sat on him was called Faithful and True, and in righteousness He judges and makes war. . . . And the armies in heaven, clothed in fine linen, white and clean, followed Him on white horses. . . . And He has on His robe and on His thigh a name written: KING OF KINGS AND LORD OF LORDS (Revelation 19:11, 14, 16).

Jesus is our Savior, Redeemer, Lord, and coming King. He is the Hope of the ages. He is this world's rightful Ruler. The day is fast approaching when He will sit upon the throne of this world and reign righteously forever. You and I can live in His kingdom in peace forever.

But meanwhile there are more end-time signs to be discovered. We will explore them in the next chapter.

Endnotes

[1] This prophecy was fulfilled in A.D. 70, when Roman troops under the command of their general, Titus, attacked Jerusalem, devastating the city and destroying the temple.

[2] "Cult Questions and Answers," Cult Hotline & Clinic, http://www.cultclinic.org/qa2.html.

[3] Milton Leitenberg, "Deaths in Wars and Conflicts in the 20th Century," (Cornell University Peace Studies Program, occasional paper 29, 3rd ed., 2006), http://www.cissm.umd.edu/papers/files/deathswarsconflictsjune52006.pdf.

Chapter 3

More Signs of His Coming

The hurricane that struck New England on September 21, 1938, was the worst in the region's history. As a boy growing up in southern Connecticut, I frequently heard old-time New Englanders describe the fury of that monster storm. They vividly told of flooded cities, destroyed buildings, fallen trees, and lost lives.

An extensive report on the storm's massive destruction prepared by the Coastal and Hydraulics Laboratory, a Department of Defense research unit, states,

> The winds grew gradually during the morning of the 21st, and through the afternoon and evening, 80–100 mph winds crushed houses, knocked down trees, and lifted barges and boats onto land. Throughout New York and New England, the wind and water felled 275 million trees, seriously damaged more than 200,000 buildings, knocked trains off their tracks, and beached thousands of boats. Damage from the storm was estimated at $600 million. This value is in 1938 dollars; multiplying by 10 provides an estimate in present currency. Considering that wind and rain damage extended as far north as Rutland, Vermont, that entire city blocks burned in New London and other industrial towns, and that downtown Providence, Hartford, and other cities were flooded, if this storm were to occur today, the cost of the damage wrought would be staggering.[1]

Everett S. Allen's *A Wind to Shake the World: The Story of the 1938 Hurricane*[2] tells the saga of one New Englander who lived through it.

> On the day of the hurricane, a Yankee farmer received a package containing a barometer that he had ordered through the mail. No matter how many times he tapped it, the mercury remained stuck at the bottom of the glass. Finally, he re-packaged the "broken" barometer and returned it to the post office. By the time he got back to his own property, his house had washed out to sea.[3]

The old farmer failed to trust the very instrument that he had purchased to warn him of such a storm. He thought the barometer must be broken, and how could he trust a "broken barometer"?

Millions of people today are missing the signs Jesus is giving us as wake-up calls so we'll prepare for His return. These people have failed to discern the omens around them. They rush through life so absorbed with the things of our time that they are totally unaware that we are living in the time of the end, on the verge of eternity. In the previous chapter, we studied some of the signs in the religious and political world that Jesus gave to remind His people of the nearness of His return. In this chapter, we will especially notice the signs Jesus predicted would occur in nature and society just before the climax of human history. We will also consider the final end-time sign—the one that will immediately precede Jesus' second coming.

Nature gone wild

The Bible predicts that all nature will be out of control just before the coming of Jesus. We should expect tornadoes, fires, floods, and hurricanes—an epidemic of destruction that we can hardly imagine.

The Bible's list of natural disasters includes worldwide famine and the hunger it brings. Jesus said, "There will be famines, pestilences, and earthquakes in various places" (Matthew 24:7). His statement raises some pertinent questions. Haven't we always had famines? Haven't there always been hungry children?

The answer, of course, is Yes, there have always been hungry children. Hunger is nothing new. But here is the difference. Jesus didn't predict a single famine. He said there would be "famines" plural—famines on an international scale; hunger of an unprecedented magnitude—just before His return. Even a casual glance at what's happening around the world reveals that His words are being fulfilled. The graphic images flashing across our TV screens of gaunt, malnourished children awaken us to the fulfillment of prophecy. The United Nations reported that thirty-five countries of the world require major food assistance, twenty-eight of which are in Africa.[4]

Most of those who live in the West have full bellies, and they're troubled by obesity rather than starvation, so it's difficult for us to believe that the kind of hunger our Lord said there would be just before His return actually does exist now. When we're surrounded by fast-food restaurants and convenience stores, it's hard for us to picture children whose stomachs are crying out for food. In spite of all the money that goes to provide aid to developing countries, the statistics on hunger are staggering. One-seventh of the world's population, almost a billion people, will go hungry today. More than sixteen thousand children per day—six million each year—die of starvation. The world produces enough food for everyone, but limited access and rising prices cause devastating shortages. Jesus' prediction regarding famine is coming true with uncanny accuracy. The only hope is the coming of the Lord.

Many are concerned by another disturbing trend. As the population of the world is growing, much arable agricultural land is being lost. Through improper land management, environmental disasters, and urban growth, more than one hundred thousand square kilometers of arable land—that's millions of acres—is lost for agricultural use each year. More than sixty countries of the world now have less than 5 percent of their land available for growing food.[5]

After Jesus listed famines, He added that there would also be pestilences (see verse 7). A pestilence is something that afflicts some form of life—especially if that ultimately results in something bad happening to us. Pestilences can have natural causes, or they can be triggered by the carelessness of human beings.

Matthew 24 says that in the end time there will be famines and pestilences. This prophecy is rapidly being fulfilled. You've probably read or heard news reports about the misuse of pesticides on our crops, which results in threats to our health. Farmers feel they have to put so many chemicals on their crops because of the increase in the number of strains of insects and disease that destroy them. Pestilences are spreading rapidly in various parts of the world.

Another form of pestilence is the increasing number of disease epidemics—new and old—that are springing up around the world. For example, we hear of mad cow disease, bird flu, HIV/AIDS, the Marburg virus, and lyme disease. And while medical researchers are working diligently and faithfully to bring one disease under control, another one breaks out somewhere else. Here again we see a fulfillment of the prophecies of Jesus Christ.

Another cause of pestilence is pollution of the environment. United Nations reports tell us that as much as twenty-one billion pounds of toxic substances pollute the world each year, causing thousands of premature deaths.[6] Our air, our land, and our waterways are polluted. Our oceans and forests are rapidly being destroyed, and often our food itself is tainted by toxic chemicals. Back in 1992, 104 Nobel Prize–winning scientists and an additional fifteen hundred internationally known scientists signed a document titled "World Scientists' Warning to Humanity," which declared, "No more than one or a few decades remain before the chance to avert the new threats we now confront will be lost and the prospects of humanity immeasurably diminished."[7]

Earthquakes

Jesus continued the list of the signs of His coming that we can see in the natural world. He said, "There will be famines, pestilences, *and earthquakes in various places*" (verse 7; emphasis added). In other words, the Bible predicts that there will be "a whole lot of shaking going on" just before the coming of Jesus!

The book of Revelation tells us about the greatest earthquake that will ever trouble this planet. The apostle John saw that one in a vision. He said that when it hit, "there were noises and thunderings and lightnings; and there was a great earthquake, such a mighty and great earthquake as had not occurred since men were on the earth" (Revelation 16:18). This earthquake, the most powerful ever to shake the earth, will occur at the coming of Jesus. But previous to its striking, thousands of earthquakes all over the world will foretell Jesus' return. These earthquakes will come in rapid succession and without any warning. Do you find this hard to believe? Well, according to reliable estimates, this planet already experiences an average of fifty-five earthquakes per day, or twenty thousand per year.[8]

"There will be great earthquakes in various places, and famines and pestilences; and there will be fearful sights and great signs from heaven" (Luke 21:11). This upheaval in nature will reveal itself in various ways. Hurricanes, typhoons, and tornadoes will manifest themselves in rapid succession. And "men's hearts [will fail] them from fear and the expectation of those things which are coming on the earth" (verse 26).

Think of it! People clutching their children, their homes destroyed, and wondering, "What do I do next? Where do I go from here?" But as Christians, we have hope in Jesus. He will strengthen us to face the challenges of today and the crisis at the close of this earth's history. For

God is our refuge and strength, a very present help in

trouble. Therefore we will not fear, even though the earth be removed, and though the mountains be carried into the midst of the sea; though its waters roar and be troubled, though the mountains shake with its swelling (Psalm 46:1–3).

When it appears that all of nature is out of control, God is still on top of things. Our faith need not be shaken when the earth is quaking. Hurricanes, tornadoes, earthquakes, famines, fires, and floods will strike with increasing frequency and unexpected suddenness. It will seem as though all of the earth is crying out for deliverance. A line that the apostle Paul wrote will ring true to the generation that witnesses this: "We know that the whole creation groans and labors with birth pangs together until now" (Romans 8:22). Through it all, God will not desert us. He'll be there for us. As the old song says, "Just when I need Him, Jesus is near. . . . Just when I need Him most."

Recently, our world has experienced major tsunamis. Two of the most powerful ever to strike the earth since records have been kept struck during the past decade. The tsunami that struck on December 26, 2004, which was precipitated by an earthquake that registered 9.1 on the Richter scale, killed more than 230,000 people almost instantly, and the damage it did is indescribable. Hundreds of thousands were made homeless, and relief efforts couldn't keep up with the incredible human need.[9]

And on Friday, March 11, 2011, a 9.0 magnitude earthquake struck off the east coast of Japan. As far as we know, it was the most powerful earthquake ever to hit Japan, and it was one of the five most powerful earthquakes on earth since modern record-keeping began in 1900. The earthquake triggered huge, powerful waves in the ocean—waves that reached heights of up to 133 feet and traveled up to six miles inland.

On March 12, 2012, a Japanese National Police Agency report

confirmed 15,861 people killed, 6,107 injured, and 2,939 missing, as well as 130,429 buildings totally collapsed, with a further 262,818 buildings "half collapsed," and another 691,766 buildings partially damaged.[10] A report from a United Nations disaster risk reduction agency put the economic cost at US$210 billion, making it the most expensive natural disaster in history.[11]

In the passage of Luke quoted above, Jesus also spoke of fearful sights in the heavens. In the hurricane season of 2005, the Atlantic Ocean spawned more storms large enough to be named than ever before. Hurricane Katrina was the costliest storm in American history, producing $108 billion in damage.[12] And the rash of tornadoes the United States has had in the 2008–2012 seasons has left town after town devastated. This unprecedented plague of tornadoes has inflicted billions of dollars of damage on communities.

The increased frequency of these natural disasters is a sign of the return of our Lord. All the earth is crying out, "Oh, Jesus, come soon." Mother Earth is having labor pains. Soon Jesus will come, not as a babe in Bethlehem's manger, but as earth's rightful Ruler and King of kings and Lord of lords. The signs we see in the natural world are not to frighten us. They are signposts of hope that shout loudly that we are almost home.

But remember, no one sign, no single event, tells us He's coming immediately. When we see *all* of the signs our Lord foretold occurring around the whole world and with increased frequency, we can know for certain that His coming is near.

Society's signs

So far, we've looked at what the Bible says regarding the signs of Jesus coming that will be seen in the areas of religion, politics, and nature. Now let's look at His predictions regarding society in general.

Our Lord predicted that the moral fabric of society would fall apart just before His return. Moral decay, corruption, and violence would swamp the whole earth. He said, "As the days of Noah were, so also will the coming of the Son of Man be. For . . . in the days before the flood, they were eating and drinking, marrying and giving in marriage, until the day that Noah entered the ark" (Matthew 24:37, 38).

What's wrong with eating and drinking? What's wrong with marrying and giving in marriage? Nothing, of course—unless people fill their lives with these things and leave no room for God. This passage describes a population that continued living self-centered, godless lives when this world was on the verge of destruction by the Flood. Pleasure dominated their lives, and they ignored the signs of the times.

Noah proclaimed, "A flood is coming," but the people of his day were so absorbed in the routine of their lives that they considered him to be a wild-eyed fanatic. They weren't moved spiritually. They didn't repent of their sins. They were engrossed in the here and now. Their minds were absorbed in the things of this life, which crowded eternity out of their thinking.

Jesus predicted the same attitudes would be prevalent just before His second coming. Though we're living on the verge of eternity, most people are consumed with the here and now to the exclusion of living godly lives.

Jesus also predicted that the last days would be characterized by waning morality. When the Savior says "as the days of Noah were," He's telling us that the spiritual condition of the society prevalent on earth just before His return will be similar to that of Noah's day, which God felt was so evil that it—and the world in which it existed—must be destroyed. The Bible's first book, Genesis, provides insight on "the days of Noah." It says, "The LORD saw that the wickedness of man was great in the earth, and that every intent of his heart was only evil continually. . . . The earth also was corrupt before God, and the earth was filled with violence" (Genesis 6:5, 11).

Let's look at some incredible statistics regarding births to unmarried women in America today. More than 40 percent of the children born in the United States are born to unmarried women, and the rate skyrockets to 88 percent of children born to women fifteen to nineteen years old.[13] In the United States over the past forty years, about 67 percent of marriages have failed.[14] The U.S. Census Bureau's 2010 report shows that 50 percent of all United States households are headed by unmarried people.[15]

And this trend is spreading rapidly around the world. The biblical model of the family is being shattered in twenty-first-century society. More countries are accepting same-sex marriage as being just as valid as the biblical model of marriage between one man and one woman. What a tragedy that love has degenerated into lust! What a tragedy that divorce rates are so often leaving the children lost in confusion and devastation.

But there is hope. Whatever blows life has dealt you, and whatever circumstances you find yourself in, God is there, and He can work a miracle in your life. He is the God of new beginnings. He can give you a new sense of His love and care. He will put His arms around you. He offers you a new future. No matter what mistakes you have made, God will forgive you and give you a new start. The message God sent through Jeremiah is especially meant for you:

> I know the thoughts that I think toward you, says the LORD, thoughts of peace and not of evil, to give you a future and a hope. Then you will call upon Me and go and pray to Me, and I will listen to you (Jeremiah 29:11, 12).

Another aspect of this passage is the unprecedented violence in our world. The social fabric of society is falling apart. We live in a world of increasing crime and violence. Mass media has brought these evils into our homes in frightening ways. Action games played by very young children are filled with violence. Even cartoons that used to provide what some believed to be innocent entertainment are now characterized by graphic violence. Some estimate that the average twelve-year-old boy has witnessed, in television shows, fourteen thousand murders! Researchers are still trying to grasp how this increased dose of violence has affected the developing consciences of these boys.

Violence has become a global concern. The World Health Organization has revealed just how great a problem it is on a global scale. The first-ever world report on violence has produced some shocking statistics.[16] "Each year, more than 1.6 million people worldwide lose their lives to violence. . . . Many more are injured and suffer from a range of physical, sexual, reproductive, and mental health problems. Violence is among the leading causes of death for people aged 15–44 years worldwide, accounting for about 14 percent of deaths among males and 7 percent of deaths among females."[17]

What's happening in our world today seems to be a reflection of the Genesis account of the epidemic of violence at the time of the Flood. The biblical description of Noah's day echoes in our ears: "The earth also was corrupt before God, and the earth was filled with violence" (Genesis 6:11).

The Bible also lists economic uncertainty as a sign of the last days. James, the brother of Jesus, describes the economic condition of our world before Jesus comes this way:

> Come now, you rich, weep and howl for your miseries that are coming upon you! Your riches are corrupted, and your garments are moth-eaten. Your gold and silver are corroded, and their corrosion will be a witness against you and will eat your flesh like fire. You have heaped up treasure in the last days (James 5:1–3).

Revelation's end-time prophecies add even more detail to the economic conditions just before the return of our Lord. Apparently there will be a sudden collapse of the world's economy. "The merchants of the earth will weep and mourn over her [Babylon], for no one buys their merchandise anymore. . . . 'For in one hour such great riches came to nothing' " (Revelation 18:11, 17).

As I write these words the United States is drowning in debt, which is approaching a staggering sixteen trillion dollars.[18] This is equivalent to more than fifty thousand dollars for every American citizen! Americans owe approximately eight hundred billion dollars in personal credit-card debt, and the amount is growing every day.[19]

We are not alone in our debt crisis. Europe is staggering under the heavy burden of debt as well. The monetary systems of Greece, Spain, and Italy are teetering on the verge of collapse. France and England, once the stalwarts of the European economy, are suffering as well. One thing is certain: no society can continually run up its national and personal debt without one day collapsing economically. The handwriting is on the wall. We are headed for economic disaster. But hope is on the way.

However, before we get to that hope, we must consider carefully two more signs. First, an angel told the prophet Daniel that he was to "shut up the words, and seal the book until the time of the end . . . [when] many shall run to and fro, and knowledge shall increase" (Daniel 12:4).

Anyone who thinks knowledge has not increased is sleeping through the digital age. The amount of knowledge we have is growing at an explosive rate. When my three-year-old granddaughter teaches me about her iPad, I am convinced that knowledge is increasing! A few years ago, those who wanted to communicate with people on the other side of the world would write a letter with a fountain pen or a typewriter and send it on a several-day-long journey through the mail. Now we send and receive gigabytes of information anywhere in the world instantly. Knowledge is being increased dramatically.

More than 90 percent of all the scientists and technicians that ever lived are living today. Every time you turn on your computer, check your messages on your iPhone, read a book on your Kindle, or play a game on your iPad, you testify that knowledge is indeed increasing at an exponential rate. It is also quite amazing that the gadgets we think are so brilliantly designed today will be out of date in six months when the next model is introduced into the marketplace.

But when the angel was speaking to Daniel about an explosion of knowledge, he was speaking of something much more important than intellectual knowledge, more important than scientific knowledge. He was talking about a knowledge of the the prophecies of Scripture and especially of the end-time prophecies of Daniel. Just before the return of our Lord, the gospel will be proclaimed powerfully in all the world. The earth will be illuminated with the knowledge of the glory of God (Revelation 18:1).

The final sign

There's one more sign—the final sign. When we see it, we'll know that we are almost home. We're on the verge of the coming of Jesus. How will we know that Jesus' coming is near? We'll know when we see that the gospel is being preached in all the world.

The apostle John said "the everlasting gospel" would be preached "to every nation, tribe, tongue, and people" of "those who dwell on the earth" (Revelation 14:6). And Jesus said that when the "gospel of the kingdom" is "preached in all the world as a witness to all the nations, . . . *then the end will come*" (Matthew 24:14; emphasis added). So when we see the gospel being proclaimed around the world, we know that the end is near.

In order to finish His work on earth in our day, God is using multiple ways of communicating. He is "not willing that any should perish," and He "desires all mankind to be saved and come to a knowledge of the truth" (2 Peter 3:9; 1 Timothy 2:4). Think about it for a moment. Living as we do in the twenty-first century, we have the most sophisticated communication systems in the history of this world. Through massive global radio networks, international television systems, giant publishing houses, instant Internet connections, and a global satellite communication system, this world is linked as one global village. What happens in one part of the world is known almost instantly in another part of the world thousands of miles away. Even totalitarian regimes, despotic rulers, and intolerant governments are powerless to stop the transmission of the gospel. God is in this. He is using the advance in communication as a vehicle through which to share the gospel with every person on the planet.

Prophecy is being fulfilled. In the former Communist lands, God is working miracles. The Berlin Wall has crumbled. The Iron Curtain has come down. Many totalitarian regimes are no more. God is doing amazing things throughout eastern Europe and the former U.S.S.R. The gospel is going forward in power, and tens of thousands are responding to God's final call.

God is also opening doors in China that have been closed for years. According to a news story in *Foreign Policy,*

> Amid growing social tension and an ominous economic outlook, some quarters of the officially atheist Chinese Communist Party seem to be warming to Christianity. Land is being donated, churches built, and research being conducted on positive Christian contributions—all by the Chinese government, which until recently treated religion as a harmful but unstoppable force.[20]

Although it is impossible to know the exact number of Christians in China today, most experts on the subject believe there are at least sixty million. In one area of northeast China, more than three thousand people were baptized in a single three-day period in one church district. There are more Christians in church each week in China than in the whole of Europe. Christianity is growing explosively there.

And then there's India, a country that has resisted the preaching of the gospel for centuries. Early Christian missionaries worked there for decades with only a few converts to show for their labors. But there is a new receptivity to the gospel in India today.

Thousands are coming to Jesus and being baptized. Former Hindus are becoming Christians. In one section of northern India, more than one hundred thousand have accepted Jesus. People in village after village are begging for someone to tell them about Jesus.

God is on the move. Prophecy is being fulfilled. God's Holy Spirit is being poured out. The gospel is going to the world. And now a spiritual revival is taking place on the continent of Africa. God is doing something unusual, and as a result, tens of thousands are being baptized into Jesus Christ and committing themselves to following His Word.

Certainly there are areas resistant to the gospel—places where millions of people have yet to hear God's words of truth. The major cities of this world, the Islamic Middle East, and the major non-Christian religions elsewhere still pose formidable challenges to our proclaiming the gospel to *all* the world in this generation. But it is obvious that God is on the move, and through the outpouring of His mighty Holy Spirit, He will accomplish what seems impossible. The gospel will be proclaimed to the ends of the earth. In earth's final hour, every person on the planet will have the opportunity to accept Jesus' last-day message.

God is fulfilling His Word. We are on the verge of the kingdom. The signs that our Lord gave are being fulfilled.

It is the midnight hour, and God is appealing to men and women. He is appealing to you and me to be ready for His return.

Endnotes

[1] "The Great New England Hurricane of 1938," Coastal and Hydraulics Laboratory, http://chl.wes.army.mil/shore/newyork/longisland/1938hurricane.pdf.

[2] Everett S. Allen, *A Wind to Shake the World: The Story of the 1938 Hurricane* (New York: Little, Brown, 1976).

[3] Allen, *A Wind to Shake the World;* quoted in the September 21, 2003, entry of "River of Dreams," Doug Simpson's Web log (see www.dougsimpson.com/river/archives/0001129.html.)

[4] "World Food Stocks to Rise, but Hunger Persists in Sahel Region, Middle East—UN Report," UN News Centre, June 13, 2012, http://www.un.org/apps/news/story.asp?NewsID=42215&Cr=Food&Cr1=.

[5] "Geography Statistics: Land Use, Arable Land (Most Recent) by Country," Nationmaster.com, http://www.nationmaster.com/graph/geo_lan_use_ara_lan-geography-land-use-arable.

[6] "Toxic Chemicals Released by Industry This Year," Worldometers.info, http://www.worldometers.info/view/toxchem/.

[7] Henry Kendall, "World Scientists' Warning to Humanity," November 18, 1992, transcript available at http://www.worldtrans.org/whole/warning.html and several other reputable Web sites.

[8] "FAQs—Earthquake Myths," U.S. Geological Survey Earthquake Hazards Program, last modified October 27, 2009, http://earthquake.usgs.gov/learn/faq/?categoryID=6&faqID=110.

[9] "Tsunami Report Criticises Relief Effort," *Guardian,* October 5, 2005, http://www.guardian.co.uk/world/2005/oct/05/internationalaidanddevelopment.tsunami2004.

[10] "Damage Situation and Police Countermeasures Associated With 2011 Tohoku District—Off the Pacific Ocean Earthquake, June 13, 2012," National Police Agency of Japan, http://www.npa.go.jp/archive/keibi/biki/higaijokyo_e.pdf.

[11] "Disasters Cost $380 Billion in 2011, Says UN," AFP, March 5, 2012, http://bit.ly/yEgflJ.

[12] Richard D. Knabb, Jamie R. Rhome, and Daniel P. Brown, "Tropical Cyclone Report, Hurricane Katrina, 23-30 August 2005," National Hurricane Center, December 20, 2005, http://www.nhc.noaa.gov/pdf/TCR-AL122005_Katrina.pdf.

[13] "In 2010, more than four in ten births (41 percent) were to unmarried women." Child Trends Data Bank, last updated March 2012, http://www.childtrendsdatabank.org/?q=node/196.

[14] John Gottman and Nan Silver, *The Seven Principles for Making Marriage Work* (New York: Three Rivers Press, 1999), 4.

[15] *U.S. Census Bureau, Statistical Abstract of the United States: 2012,* 55, http://www.census.gov/compendia/statab/2012/tables/12s0063.pdf. This figure includes single mothers (by far the largest group) and single fathers; those

who married and then divorced; those who never married; cohabiting couples; families composed of siblings living together; and the widowed.

[16] Etienne G. Krug, Linda L. Dahlberg, James A. Mercy, Anthony B. Zwi, and Rafael Lozano, eds., *World Report on Violence and Health* (Geneva: World Health Organization, 2002).

[17] "I'm Playing Hide and Seek," World Health Organization "Explaining Away Violence" poster series, http://www.who.int/violence_injury_prevention /violence/global_campaign/en/PostExpGeneral.pdf.

[18] See http://www.usdebtclock.org/.

[19] See http://www.creditcards.com/credit-card-news/credit-card-industry -facts-personal-debt-statistics-1276.php.

[20] Eric Fish, "China's 'Come to Jesus' Moment," *Foreign Policy,* February 15, 2012, http://www.foreignpolicy.com/articles/2012/02/15/china_christian _awakening.

Chapter 4

The Surprise of a Lifetime

She was the pride of the twenty-two-ship Townsend Thoresen fleet—a magnificent vessel christened the *Herald of Free Enterprise*. The ship ferried passengers and vehicles across the English Channel in first-class comfort. At 433 feet long and a displacement of about eight thousand tons, she could weather most any storm.

And yet, on the night of March 6, 1987, the passengers on the *Herald* experienced a terrifying surprise, one in which 193 men, women, and children lost their lives in a matter of seconds. How could such a tragedy happen just because someone forgot to close a couple of doors?

Everything about the ship's preparations for the crossing from Belgium to England went routinely. The crew had done it all countless times before. The *Herald of Free Enterprise* was a RORO—a roll-on, roll-off ferry. Hundreds of vehicles and passengers could come aboard very quickly through the massive steel doors in the bow of the ship.

At 7:05 P.M. on that gray winter evening, the *Herald* began backing out of her dock at Zeebrugge Harbor. The sea was calm, and the easterly wind light.

Loading officer Leslie Sabel stood at a control panel on G deck, where the vehicles were parked. Across the dimly lit deck, he spotted someone in orange overalls weaving between the cars and trucks toward the bow. He thought it was Mark Stanley, the crewmember whose job it was to close the twelve-ton, hydraulically operated bow doors. Satisfied that the job would be done, Sabel climbed a stairway toward the bridge.

Stanley, however, was in his quarters—fast asleep. Like the rest of the crew, he was working a twenty-four-hour shift. That afternoon, after doing some maintenance, he had decided to make himself some tea in his cabin. Then, feeling very tired, he sat down on his bunk, opened a book—and fell asleep almost immediately. And he slept through the call to harbor stations.

The captain of the ship, David Lewry, might have noticed that the bow doors were still open—bright dockside lights were shining on them, and they were just visible below the bridge. But he was backing the ship out of her berth, so the captain was facing the stern. And by the time the *Herald* swung around, she was in darkness.

At 7:20 P.M., the ship accelerated into the main shipping channel, and a bow wave began to pile up under her blunt prow. As the *Herald* continued to pick up speed, churning white water broke over the top of the car deck, rushing in at the rate of two hundred tons per minute. The vehicle deck ran from one end of the ship to the other, so there was nothing to interrupt the flow of the sea into the *Herald*.

While the vehicle deck was flooding, most of the passengers were sitting in the restaurants on board, lining up at the duty-free shop, or relaxing comfortably in the lounges, chatting or dozing off. Everyone was feeling quite warm and safe. But at 7:27 P.M., the *Herald* began to roll over on its port side. While the crew and passengers wondered what on earth was going on, the ship righted itself briefly and then rolled completely onto its side. Seawater rushed in through windows in the upper decks, and the ship began to sink. Those who weren't crushed to death or drowned tried to climb to safety, clutching at lighting fixtures and ledges as they tried to work their way to what was now the top of the ship.

What happened so suddenly to the *Herald* that night was the worst British peacetime marine disaster since the sinking of the *Iolaire* in 1919. It was completely unexpected. In a matter of seconds, the world inside the *Herald* had been completely upset. In one instant, passengers were chewing on deli sandwiches, and in the next they were crashing through tables toward the port side. In one instant, passengers were paying for souvenirs, and in the next they were wrenched away by a rush of icy seawater. How could anyone be prepared for that?

Caught by surprise

The Bible speaks of another event soon to happen that many people will consider to be a disaster. Events in the world today are building up to the great climax of history. For some people, that will be a glorious event, but it will strike others with all the terror raised by thieves breaking into their homes at midnight. Notice how the apostle Paul describes it: "You yourselves know perfectly that the day of the Lord so comes as a thief in the night. For when they say, 'Peace and safety!' then sudden destruction comes upon them, as labor pains upon a pregnant woman. And they shall not escape" (1 Thessalonians 5:2, 3).

What is this "day of the Lord"? It's the second coming of Jesus Christ. It's the promised return of our Lord. He said He was leaving so He could prepare a place in heaven for His followers, and He promised that He would come back to take them there.

Some people will see the Second Coming as a glorious event. But for others, it will be as welcome as the midnight break-in of thieves.

It doesn't have to be the latter. Your world doesn't have to turn upside down when Jesus comes. It can, in fact, turn right side up. Look at the rest of this passage in 1 Thessalonians:

> But you, brethren, are not in darkness, so that this Day should overtake you as a thief. You are all sons of light and sons of the day. We are not of the night nor of darkness. Therefore let us not sleep, as others do, but let us watch and be sober (verses 4–6).

People who have made a commitment to Jesus Christ, the Light of the world, are called children of light. They're not groping about in the dark anymore. They have a Friend who guides them toward a secure future. They have the assurance that Jesus is returning to take them to their eternal home. When Jesus returns, they will shout with joy, "Behold, this is our God; we have waited for Him, and He will save us. This is the Lord; we have waited for Him; we will be glad and rejoice in His salvation" (Isaiah 25:9). What is a terrifying surprise to the unsaved people of this world is reason for gladness and rejoicing to those who have committed their lives to Jesus.

So, Paul says, if you belong to the day, don't fall asleep spiritually. Stay awake. Watch and be sober. Or, as other translations put it, "Be alert and self-controlled."

When Jesus returns, He will appear like a thief in the night only to those who are sleeping. To those who are awake, He will appear as a wonderful Friend and Savior. So it matters a great deal whether we're spiritually asleep or awake at the second coming of Jesus Christ. That's an important event. The eternal destiny of every human being who has ever lived will be decided. It's one of the things that matters most in life.

Let's look at the reason people start falling asleep spiritually—especially as it relates to Jesus' return to earth. First of all, a lot of time has passed since Jesus promised to come back. Two thousand years is a long time to be in the waiting mode, so it's easy for people to forget about Jesus' return or push it into the distant future—allowing the present to become so full of duties and responsibilities that the eternal is crowded out.

Time crowds out eternity.

The problems of today crowd out the joy of tomorrow.

The cares of the moment crowd out our hopes for the future.

Interestingly enough, the Bible anticipated this state of mind. It anticipated what would happen when people thought the coming of Jesus was delayed. Jesus told the story of ten bridesmaids who were waiting for a wedding to begin. According to Him, "while the bridegroom was delayed, they all slumbered and slept" (Matthew 25:5).

The coming of the bridegroom caught both the wise and the foolish bridesmaids by surprise. The difference between the two classes isn't that the wise were wide awake and the foolish were sleeping. It is that the wise were prepared and the foolish were not.

Here's the picture. Time passes. Everything appears to be fairly normal. Life seems to be continuing on in its regular routine—and then the unexpected happens. Look at how the apostle Peter describes it: "Scoffers will come in the last days . . . saying, 'Where is the promise of His coming? For since the fathers fell asleep, all things continue as they were from the beginning of creation' " (2 Peter 3:3, 4).

"All things continue." People see the seasons coming and going as the years pass. The pattern never changes. Generations come and go; human life goes on. It's hard to imagine any big supernatural interruption.

And they have a point. Sometimes it is hard to imagine Jesus bursting through the heavens.

So what's Peter's answer to the scoffers? What assurance does he offer us?

He says that these skeptics are forgetting one important thing— that the Creator fashioned the heavens above us and made the earth below us. That He once covered the world with a flood.

What's Peter's point? Well, he's getting at the real issue behind all the skepticism and doubt. The real issue is, Who's in charge? Who's ultimately controlling history?

When things go on and on and stay pretty much the same, it's easy to assume that we're in charge. We unconsciously move God out of the picture. He's out there in some other dimension, we think, not really sovereign over this planet.

So Peter says, "Just stop and think about who made all this. God created this planet—and the whole universe—by His word. It all came about at His command. The One who began it all is quite capable of ending it all. His word is still powerful." In effect, Peter is saying, "Think about it. All human history had a beginning point.

God created this world. And this earth as we know it will have an ending point. Jesus will come again."

Peter actually does go on to explicitly make this point in this passage. He says,

> But the heavens and the earth which are now preserved by the same word, are reserved for fire until the day of judgment and perdition of ungodly men.
>
> But, beloved, do not forget this one thing, that with the Lord one day is as a thousand years, and a thousand years as one day. The Lord is not slack concerning His promise, as some count slackness, but is longsuffering toward us, not willing that any should perish but that all should come to repentance (verses 7–9).

God is not just slacking off. His coming is delayed in love. He's passionate about rescuing lost people, bringing people to a saving knowledge of His grace. He doesn't want to lose one single human being. He is long-suffering. In this long night of sin and agony, He would rather suffer Himself than lose one human being who might have been saved had He waited a little longer.

We may not understand the divine timetable. We may not see how things work from an eternal perspective in which a thousand years is like one day. But we can know this—God is working to rescue human beings, and that rescue will climax in the second coming of Jesus Christ.

Peter believes that we can be as sure of that as we can be sure that there's a sky above us and an earth beneath us. But people forget that. They forget about the Creator. They forget about the promise—it was made so long ago. And they start falling asleep spiritually.

Falling asleep spiritually

How do you fall asleep spiritually? How does that happen? Well, first of all, you're lulled to sleep by routine—the daily grind, the weekly schedule. These things start capturing all of our attention.

What happened aboard the *Herald of Free Enterprise* is instructive. Opening and closing those bow doors was so routine. Crew members had done it scores of times. No one was alert. No one made absolutely sure the doors were closed.

Routine lulls us to sleep. We get up, go to work, return home, watch some TV, make a few phone calls, and go to sleep. We get enough food in our bellies; and we provide for our families. We relax on the weekends and maybe attend church. Often, we have enough of a religious experience to make us comfortable but not enough to transform our lives. It's easy to forget what genuine spirituality really is. We just let it slide. It becomes less and less real, less and less important. Routine lulls us to sleep.

Jesus warned about this very problem. He said,

> As in the days before the flood, they were eating and drinking, marrying and giving in marriage, until the day that Noah entered the ark, and did not know until the flood came and took them all away, so also will the coming of the Son of Man be (Matthew 24:38, 39).

There's nothing wrong with eating and drinking and marrying. They're good things. They're healthy things. But if that's all we're doing, then the Flood, the end, will take us by surprise. Caught up in the pressure of little things, little duties, we forget about the big things, the big duties. We don't close the doors, and the flood pours in.

On the *Herald,* everyone assumed that someone else was taking care of it. Everyone was looking the other way. It was easy to fall asleep.

We make similar assumptions in the spiritual life. Someone else will take care of it. The church will take care of it. If my name is on the books, then I must have done enough to satisfy God's requirements.

The pastor will take care of it; after all, I sit through his sermons. I put in my time in the pew. That ought to take care of my spiritual needs.

Who's making absolutely sure that the doors are closed? That's up to each individual. We have to take that responsibility. No one else's spirituality is going to save us in the end.

When the frigid waters of the English Channel rushed into the *Herald* and that huge ship rolled over on its side, passengers were thrown in all directions. A young couple, Susan and Rob, had just ordered dinner when it happened. They were sitting just a few feet apart at the table. Both clutched at the furnishings as the ship rolled. Both were stunned when the water rushed over them.

But Susan tumbled underwater to a passageway. She managed to grab a shelf and hang onto it till she was rescued.

Rob didn't make it. Susan never saw him again.

That's the way it went. Two other people were sitting side by side in the lounge. One was thrown out a window by the water and rose up to safety; the other was crushed in the debris. Two people were walking on an upper deck. One clutched a stairway rail and clambered up to rescuers; the other missed a handhold by inches and fell into the deep. Destinies were decided in a few seconds.

Something like what happened on the *Herald of Free Enterprise* is going to happen at the second coming of Jesus Christ. He said that at His coming "two men will be in the field; one will be taken and the other left. Two women will be grinding with a hand mill; one will be taken and the other left" (verses 40, 41, NIV). Jesus' very next words were, "Therefore keep watch" (verse 42, NIV).

Why is one taken and the other left? Because one is sleeping and the other is awake.

"What?" someone says. "Jesus said the two men were both working in the field, and the two women were both grinding with a hand mill. It sounds like they're doing exactly the same things."

But the point is that one in each pair is spiritually dead and the other is spiritually alive. One in each group is saved, and one in each is lost when Jesus comes. For the lost, Jesus comes like a thief in the night. For the saved, He comes as a long-awaited Friend. And there is no second chance.

Yes, there will be some heart-wrenching dramas on that day. Suddenly, the sky will seem to split open, allowing a brilliant beam of light to fall on the earth. Something like a trumpet sounds in the bursting sky—and that sound seems to circle the earth and pierce every heart. No one has ever seen anything like what will happen on that day.

Jesus is coming to earth like some brilliant satellite surrounded by what seems to be a galaxy of angels. And the coming of Jesus settles the eternal destiny of everyone living on planet Earth.

Lessons from the *Titanic*

On April 15, 2012, the world commemorated the one-hundredth anniversary of the sinking of the *Titanic*. Before the crash, there was no sign of danger. The cold, dark sea was calm—as smooth as glass beneath the star-studded heavens. It was an hour before midnight. Some people had gone to bed and slipped into a serene sleep. Others ate in the luxurious dining room or sat in the first-class lounge beneath the decks and listened as the band played soothing songs. They were totally unaware that the greatest maritime tragedy in a time of peace awaited them in the ice-strewn waters of the North Atlantic. They were totally oblivious to the fact that 1,514 people, two-thirds of all the people on that mighty ship, would be dead before the night was over.

The great steamship was an engineering masterpiece. So carefully had it been planned and constructed, with sixteen watertight compartments in a hull that was nine hundred feet long, that it is said the captain had boasted, "Not even God Himself could sink her."

The crew of the *Titanic* received multiple warnings that there were icebergs in the area. Were they so confident in their ship's ability to withstand any crash that they ignored them? Were they too busy with their routine duties to heed the messages? Were they drowsy or just plain sleepy because of the lateness of the hour? Only eternity will tell.

Whatever the case, on that starry night, the luxury liner carrying 2,223 passengers and crew struck an iceberg, which cut a gash in the ship's hull that opened five of the sixteen waterproof compartments to the icy seawater. And within a relatively short time, the "unsinkable" *Titanic* sank in the frigid waters of the North Atlantic. I think it safe to say that every person aboard the *Titanic* was surprised at the outcome. Not one of them expected the ship to sink and fifteen hundred lives to be lost.

Is Jesus' second coming going to be as much of a surprise for you as the sinking of the *Titanic* was for the people on board? Whether you are prepared for that surprise of a lifetime matters. In fact, it's one of the things that matters most. Please don't be caught sleeping on the most important day in history. Please take responsibility for your own spiritual state right now. Please don't assume someone else can take care of it. Don't be swallowed up by the routine. Make God a priority in your life right now.

Jesus urged the men and women He spoke to personally to set their priorities carefully. He admonished them to "seek first the kingdom of God and His righteousness" (Matthew 6:33). Is the kingdom of God a priority to you? Is a personal relationship with Jesus supremely important to you? Have the things of time crowded out the things of eternity, or does heaven hold first place in your heart?

You can't have a saving relationship with Jesus by chance. You have to decide to pursue it. You have to allow Jesus to come into your heart and your life. If you don't say a definite Yes to Him and do what you can to build that relationship, you'll end up sleeping, and you won't like what you'll see when you wake up.

It's so much better to wake up now. It's so much better to acknowledge now what's most important, rather than to wait until it's too late.

Chapter 5

Waiting for His Return

A Scottish philosopher named Adam Smith would sometimes get so lost in thought that he'd forget where he was. One day he got himself into quite a predicament because of his absentmindedness.

On that Sunday morning he wandered out into his backyard wearing only a nightgown. Then, totally engrossed in working out some obscure theoretical problem, he strolled out of his yard and onto the street. But he didn't stop there. He continued walking, going some fifteen miles to a neighboring town completely oblivious to everything around him.

When Smith reached that town, the loud ringing of church bells penetrated to some level of his consciousness, so he made his way into a church and took his place in a pew—still pondering. Regular churchgoers were astonished to see the philosopher in their midst clad only in his white nightgown.

Adam Smith is just one in a long line of individuals we've come to know as scholars with their head in the clouds—absentminded professors. They're never quite present, it seems, in the real world. Anecdotes about them abound.

The mathematician David Hilbert was one of them. He forgot to put on a clean shirt for a party his wife was having at their home. She quietly asked him to go upstairs and change. He went up, took off his shirt, and then, having forgotten why he was undressing, took his pants off too, and got into bed and went to sleep!

I have to confess that I'm not immune to absentmindedness. One time my wife, Teenie, asked me to go upstairs and get her glasses. While up there, I spotted a book that looked interesting, put on her glasses, and started reading. I'd forgotten all about why I went up there.

Stories about people who always have something else on their minds are amusing, but they also raise some interesting questions about the way we live every day—especially the way religious people live every day.

Are we who look forward to heaven, to the second coming of Jesus, just people with our heads in the clouds? Are we so heavenly minded that we are of no earthly good?

Are those of us who profess faith in a soon-coming Savior just absentminded professors of a different sort? Are we out of touch with reality? Are we as out of place as that absentminded philosopher sitting in a pew in his nightgown?

If Jesus really will come back to earth some day soon—how should we live *today*? That's an important question. How does Jesus' return affect how we carry on our daily lives? How should it?

The Greek philosopher Thales sheds a little light on this subject, showing us two contrasting ways of living with one's head in the clouds. Plato told about the first one.

It seems Thales was walking down a road by himself one evening, lost in contemplation, head thrown back, studying the stars, when he stumbled into a well. Brought back to reality, he started yelling for help.

A servant girl came running and pulled him out, and then said, "You're so eager to know about things in the sky that you miss what's at your own feet!"

When we live in one world while having another world in mind, we can become so focused on the far-away one that we forget where we are now.

Aristotle told a different story about Thales. He said that people sometimes taunted him, saying that his wisdom hadn't served him well; it had failed to get him any wealth. So the philosopher decided to show how useful gazing at the heavens could be. With his eyes on the skies, he bought all the olive presses in Miletus, where he lived. The harvest that year was indeed abundant, and Thales made a huge amount of money renting out his olive presses. By watching the heavens, he had learned enough about weather patterns to realize there'd be a bumper crop of olives that year. Having proven his point, he sold the presses and went back to philosophy.

So here we have two very different results from staring at the stars. On the one hand, you can stumble into a well. On the other hand, you can become incredibly prosperous. In other words, you can lose sight of reality, or you can gain a kind of wisdom that enables you to live more abundantly.

Lives of godliness and service

What does staring at the stars do for us—for you and me? More specifically, what does living in expectation of Jesus' second coming do for us? Will we stumble into a well, or will we live more abundantly?

The apostle Paul zeroed in on this issue in what is probably his earliest surviving letter, his first letter to the church in Thessalonica, in the Roman province of Macedonia. First Thessalonians is filled with the hope of the second coming of Jesus. It also takes a hard look at good and bad ways of waiting for Jesus to return. In doing that, it explodes some of the myths people had then and still have today about what it means to live with "great expectations." Let's see what insights Paul had for the Thessalonians.

We'll start with 1 Thessalonians 4. Right before a detailed passage on the hope of Jesus' coming, Paul offers a word of advice. He urges his brothers and sisters in Jesus to grow more and more in their love for one another, and he urges them to "also aspire to lead a quiet life, to mind your own business, and to work with your own hands, as we commanded you, that you may walk properly toward those who are outside, and that you may lack nothing" (1 Thessalonians 4:11, 12).

What does the apostle mean here when he tells the Thessalonians to work with their hands? Is he recommending that manual labor be the Christian norm? Is he implying we should be, say, carpenters instead of accountants?

I don't think so. Paul is simply recommending good, honest work—period. He wants believers to occupy themselves in useful labor, in taking care of the needs of their families, in setting the example of living quiet, productive lives.

Jesus pointed in the same direction in the sermon on the Second Coming that Matthew recorded in his Gospel. After graphically describing signs in the political, social, natural, and religious world just before His return, Jesus says that to be a faithful and wise servant, each one must use the gifts God has given him to bless others and build up the kingdom of God. Jesus characterizes those who take advantage of others and misuse the gifts God has given them in this time of waiting as "evil servants" (see Matthew 24:45–51).

Paul returns to this point in his second letter to the Thessalonians. He says,

> We hear that there are some who walk among you in a disorderly manner, not working at all, but are busybodies. Now those who are such we command and exhort through our Lord Jesus Christ that they work in quietness and eat their own bread. But as for you, brethren, do not grow weary in doing good (2 Thessalonians 3:11–13).

Paul calls for active waiting, not passive idleness. While we wait, we work. While we wait, we live lives of godliness and service. We do so to reveal God's character to a waiting world and a watching universe.

How should we live as we're waiting for the return of our Lord? Paul leaves no doubt: "The grace of God that brings salvation has appeared to all men, teaching us that, denying ungodliness and worldly lusts, we should live soberly, righteously, and godly in the present age, looking for the blessed hope and glorious appearing of our great God and Savior Jesus Christ" (Titus 2:11–13). Paul is saying that our great expectations ought to inspire us to live and work to please our coming King.

Fortunately, the early church took this teaching to heart. They were energized by their great expectations. They earned the admiration of the pagans by pouring out love on their neighbors. They blessed those around them. They turned the world upside down.

Hope inspires; love serves

Christians went about spreading their new faith and conquering Roman paganism. How did they do it? The early church historian Eusebius describes one reason for the rapid rise of Christianity. Eusebius says that during a plague that struck Caesarea in the fourth century,

> the evidence of the Christians' zeal and piety was made clear to all the pagans. For example, they alone in such a catastrophic state of affairs gave practical evidence of their sympathy and philanthropy by works. All day long some of them would diligently persevere in performing the last offices for the dying and burying them (for there were countless numbers, and no one to look after them). While others [i.e., Christians] gathered together in a single assemblage all who were afflicted by famine throughout the whole city, and would distribute bread to them all.
>
> When this became known, people glorified the God of the Christians, and, convinced by the deeds themselves, confessed the Christians alone were truly pious and God-fearing.[1]

Waiting for Jesus to return doesn't mean being idle. The Bible writers make that clear. If what we believe about end-time events paralyzes us instead of energizing us, then something's wrong. If we are more concerned about being saved ourselves then helping others be saved, we are missing something. If we focus upon ourselves rather than others, we're not waiting in the right way. One thing becomes very clear as you read Paul's letters to the Thessalonians. This apostle was keenly concerned with the quality of life in the here and now. He concerned himself with making life better now.

Some people fear that the more preoccupied we become with that perfect life in the hereafter, the less concern we will show for the quality of life in this world. Paul called for the exact opposite. The hope of the Second Advent floods through his letters, but it seems only to make him more passionate about getting God's qualities into people's lives now. He sums it up very nicely in 1 Thessalonians 4:3: "This is the will of God, your sanctification."

What's a good way of waiting for Jesus' return? Growing. Progressing in the spiritual life. Getting more of God's grace in our hearts. That's sanctification. So Paul frequently urged his friends to grow more and more in their love for one another. And it's evident from his letters that his love flowed out to them.

And Paul was concerned about the quality of life in the present. He showed this by tackling a particular moral problem that the Thessalonians faced.

The Thessalonians lived in a culture that turned a vice—prostitution—into a religious rite. The Greek and Roman culture of the day simply didn't reinforce sexual fidelity very strongly.

Paul was in Corinth when he wrote his letter to the Thessalonians. Corinth's patron goddess was Aphrodite. Worship of her involved wild orgies. This was the culture in which both the Corinthians and the Thessalonians were living. How should people immersed in this culture live in view of the return of the Lord Jesus Christ?

Paul spells out God's will regarding sanctification and sex:

> You should abstain from sexual immorality; that each of you should know how to possess his own vessel in sanctification and honor, not in passion of lust, like the Gentiles

who do not know God; that no one should take advantage
of and defraud his brother in this matter, because the Lord
is the avenger of all such, as we also forewarned you and
testified (1 Thessalonians 4:3–6).

Paul called believers to commit themselves to different moral
standards than their neighbors—to higher moral standards. The
quality of their life depended on doing more than just going along
with the crowd. Paul was calling them to self-control, to honorable
behavior. If we want our bodies, our sexuality, to express love rather
than lust, we must have self-control. If we are to live lives of purity
while awaiting the coming of our Lord, we must have self-control.

Act honorably in sexual matters. That was the standard Paul lifted
up in a time when promiscuity was institutionalized. He called people
to sexual fidelity. He said it clearly. It's wrong to take someone else's
spouse. It's wrong to betray the intimate bonds of marriage.

Jesus is coming again. How should we then live? We must live
with God's quality of life in mind. We're not bound to the standards
of the world around us. We're not limited to the practices of the
fickle crowd. We see another kingdom coming, and we live by its
values. We live by its standards. We are ambassadors of Jesus and
citizens of His kingdom.

Paul urged, "Walk worthy of God who calls you into His own
kingdom and glory" (1 Thessalonians 2:12).

That's the *good* way of waiting.

Trials and our Lord's return

Let's look at one characteristic of the good kind of waiting. It's
something Paul emphasized in his letters to the Thessalonians.

Some people consider the Christian hope of rescue from heaven
to be a crutch. It's for the weak. They think it's an escape—as in es-
capism. It's a way to avoid dealing with real problems.

Well, we see something quite different when we read these epistles.

In 2 Thessalonians 1:3, Paul compliments the Thessalonian believers on their faith, which, he says, "grows exceedingly," and on their love, which "abounds toward each other." And then he writes, "We ourselves boast of you among the churches of God for your patience and faith in all your persecutions and tribulations that you endure" (verse 4).

These Thessalonians were enduring persecution. Paul knew about that firsthand. His preaching had caused a riot in their city. The believers had to send him away at night because of threats on his life. (Acts 17 tells the story.)

Well, how were the Thessalonians doing in the face of tough times, opposition, and persecution? How did they do—these people who had their head in the clouds, who were so expectantly awaiting the return of Jesus? Did they wilt under pressure? Did they try to run away—to escape into some make-believe world?

No, *they stood fast*! They showed real backbone. In fact, they didn't simply *endure* in tough times, their faith and love *abounded* in tough times. They became such an example of patient strength in tribulation that Paul couldn't help boasting about them to all the other churches.

A great hope, the right kind of hope, can help us stand fast in the worst of times. It enables us to face with confidence what might otherwise intimidate us.

Hope in the return of our faithful Friend Jesus can give us inner strength. It enables us to stand fast. That's a theme that Paul carries through these epistles. The return of our Lord inspires us with hope as we face life's challenges. When difficulties surround us, we can look beyond what is to what will be. Disease, disaster, and death will not have the last word. Jesus will. One day He will gloriously descend from the heavens, and the sorrows of life will be over.

Paul tells the Thessalonians, "[I want to] encourage you concerning your faith, that no one should be shaken by these afflictions; for you yourselves know that we are appointed to this" (1 Thessalonians 3:2, 3).

We don't have to be shaken up by hard times, Paul says. We may well have to endure hardship for the sake of Jesus, but that enables us to bear witness for Him. We're part of a great cause. We have a great destiny. We're headed toward a rendezvous with the King of kings. Therefore, "stand fast," Paul urges. That's the good way of waiting. That comes from having a real hope in our hearts.

Like music in our hearts

In the mid-1960s, a brilliant young musician was becoming China's leading concert pianist. Liu Shih-kun won second prize in the Tchaikovsky Competition in Moscow—at the age of nineteen. Liu had established a worldwide reputation.

Then the Cultural Revolution swept through China. Everything Western had to be condemned. Everything "upper class" had to be renounced.

But Liu just couldn't bring himself to abandon the music he'd loved since childhood. So he was arrested as "an enemy of the people" and imprisoned.

Liu endured merciless beatings. He was totally isolated, confined in a tiny cell. He had no books to read—except for the teachings of Mao. He had no paper to write on. And most important of all to him, he had no piano. His music had been taken away from him.

Liu remained in prison for six long years. He would probably have been kept there many more years had Richard Nixon not made his historic visit to China. A new spirit of mutual respect began to blossom between the countries. And in that atmosphere, an imprisoned concert pianist became a bit of an embarrassment to the People's Republic. So, Liu was released from jail, temporarily, and asked to perform in Beijing with the Philadelphia Orchestra. The Communist officials didn't understand that a musician couldn't possibly play well after six years without a piano. Musicians have to practice every single day, or their skills soon wither away.

The day of the concert came. The frail prisoner walked onto the stage and bowed to the orchestra. He adjusted his seat at the grand piano and placed his fingertips gently on the white keys, and the music began. And incredibly, Liu Shih-kun played flawlessly, brilliantly. Western visitors who knew his story were astounded. And after Liu's final release from prison, he continued to play brilliantly—his hands flew over the keys as if they'd never stopped playing. And Liu Shih-kun was able to resume the career that had been cut off so tragically.

Liu, you see, had kept a secret from the Red Guards during his years of imprisonment. They'd taken his music away from him. They'd even denied him paper so he couldn't make any musical notations. But they couldn't take away a mind that still burned with passion and hope.

And Liu Shih-kun did practice every day of the long years he spent in that tiny prison cell. He rested his fingertips lightly on a bare cement ledge, and he played his beloved piano pieces over and over. His vivid, disciplined imagination created a keyboard no one else could see. That's why he was ready to walk out on that concert stage—out of the dark of his cell and into the bright spotlight—and perform so brilliantly.

Was Liu just another absentminded professor there, tapping away in prison? Was he just escaping from reality? I don't think so. The love of music burned in his soul. He kept alive a hope of someday playing again—on a grand piano, with a real orchestra, in a real concert. And that hope paid off.

The hope of Jesus' glorious return can keep us going—even when everything is taken away from us. Even in the worst of times. It's what keeps us practicing our faith. It's what keeps us working—quietly, faithfully, productively.

We have our minds set on the coming of a better world. Even if God's qualities are not rewarded here and now, we continue to believe in them. We still hear the music of grace and love and faith. We can keep growing toward God's quality of life. We can remain steadfast. We can endure the tiny, dark prison cell because we know that someday God will bring us into the light on a glorious stage. Someday the notes we've practiced will be played by a full orchestra—with angels singing and heavenly trumpets sounding and glorious music filling the whole sky.

Are you living productively today? Are you living God's quality of life? Are you standing fast? Are you waiting—in the good way?

Let's resolve to keep the right music alive in our hearts now. Let's resolve to keep the real hope burning bright.

Endnote

[1] Eusebius, *Ecclesiastical History,* 9.8.13, 14.

Chapter 6

Two Resurrections

It was one of the last imposing ceremonies of the Soviet Empire: the funeral of Leonid Brezhnev. The generals were all there. The escort of smart-stepping soldiers. The display of military hardware. The banners and flags.

Everything was in place to show the world how this Communist regime could honor its head of state. Everything was staged to give the impression that the Soviet Union would go on forever. Everything conformed to the script—everything but one small gesture.

It happened when Brezhnev's widow walked up to the imposing coffin. She paused a moment, and then she leaned forward and made the sign of the cross on her husband's chest.

Powerful armies and ideologies may be impressive. But when it's hope beyond the grave that we want, we have to look somewhere else.

Hope beyond the grave

These days, people are looking in all kinds of places for that hope. They're looking at Eastern religions. They're thinking that maybe becoming one with the cosmos offers a way out, or maybe reincarnation is the answer.

They're looking into the occult. Maybe we can learn something about the "other side" through contact with the dead.

They're looking at science. Some think cryogenics offers hope—having someone put our bodies in a deep freeze and thus preserving them until science discovers a way for us to live forever.

But above all, they're looking at NDEs—"near death experiences." More and more people who want some reassurance about our final journey are looking to people who've had an NDE and say they can give us a first-hand peek at life beyond the grave.

They don't have to look far. There are lots of people who claim to have had that first-hand peek, and now they're eager to tell the world what they've learned. In the popular *Saved by the Light*,[1] Dannion Brinkley claims to be sharing mysterious counsel that he received from thirteen luminous beings. And the books *Life After Life*,[2] *Recollections of Death*,[3] and *Closer to the Light*[4] offer similar insights. But few people manage to approach the popularity and influence of Betty Eadie.

Betty says that during an NDE she went to heaven and met Jesus and that He gave her many new teachings. Plenty of people have wanted to know what Betty saw in heaven. Her book *Embraced by the Light*,[5] in which she chronicled her purported experiences, stayed on the *New York Times* bestseller list for a year and a half after its publication. Since then, it has been translated into thirty-eight languages and has sold thirteen million copies in 130 countries.

Jesus, Betty says, is a benevolent Being of light. Sometimes, she says, she couldn't tell where her "light" stopped, and His began, which sounds like the New Age theme of merging or fusing with God. She also parallels New Age ideas when she speaks of having always been a part of Jesus. And in a passage that would bring mystical chills to anyone enthralled with the New Age, Betty claims that during her NDE she gazed upon a rose and "felt God in the plant, in me, his love pouring into us. We were all one."[6] If "all is one," there is no one to worship. The idea that God is in all and all are God echoes Buddhism and Hinduism.

Throughout her book Betty repeats the idea that before we were born on this earth, we existed as pre-mortal souls. And she says that when she was a preincarnate spirit, she witnessed Creation, and she claims that now her soul progresses eternally. These beliefs seem to come from the Mormonism of her youth.

Betty describes a very loving Jesus who made her feel worthy to be with Him and to embrace Him. In fact, she said His unconditional love for her overwhelmed her. This part of her story fits the picture of Jesus we find in the New Testament. But Betty had numerous other things to say that don't. For example, she concluded, based on her NDE, that Jesus is a Being completely separate from the Father. However, the Bible teaches that although Jesus is a separate and distinct Being from the Father, They are One in purpose and character. They are coequal and coeternal.

Betty concluded that she should stop regretting the bad things she had done because Jesus would do nothing to offend her. In other words, no one needs to repent for the sins he or she has committed.

Betty concluded that humans are not sinful creatures by nature. She also came to believe that human "spirit beings" assisted God at Creation and that, despite appearances, there really are no tragedies in this world. Interestingly—and importantly—salvation by grace through faith, a final judgment, and a literal second coming of Jesus are conspicuous in their absence from her writings.

Betty Eadie's NDE happened nearly twenty years before her book was published. She refuses to release her medical records, and the physician in charge when she almost died has since passed away, so there's not a lot we can check to see what really happened to her. But we *can* check what she claims Jesus told her, and when we do, we begin running into serious questions. A great deal of what Betty Eadie writes seems much closer to NDE talk than to the Bible. That is, it fits the messages other people have supposedly received through NDEs better than it does the teachings of Scripture.

The religion of the resuscitated

All the claims that people make about having enjoyed a blissful experience on "the other side" have created what one researcher calls "the religion of the resuscitated." A scene in the book *Heading Toward Omega*[7] reveals one of the key doctrines of this religion. A heavenly being who appears during an NDE consoles an anxious woman by telling her, "There are no sins." Of course, when there are no sins, there's no divine judgment and no need of salvation. Believers just "flow" into light and love.

The religion of the resuscitated doesn't focus on God so much as it does on the "unlimited potential" humans have. Betty Eadie talks of experiencing omniscience during her NDE, and she claims that now her thoughts have "tremendous power" to create reality.

Douglas Groothuis, writing in *Christianity Today*, concluded that NDE phenomena often conform to New Age beliefs that once we're freed from the fear of death and awaken to our own power, we humans can enter a glorious new consciousness.

In other words, when it comes to crossing the river to the other side, the religion of the resuscitated puts everyone in the same boat. There's no judgment, no question of personal accountability. We're all headed for the same afterlife. It's sort of a value-free eternity. We all just get into this one nice big pool of light somewhere "up there."

The Bible presents a completely different picture. The apostle Paul powerfully sets forth the biblical teaching about judgment and the afterlife.

- It is appointed for men to die once, but after this the judgment (Hebrews 9:27).
- Each of us shall give account of himself to God (Romans 14:12).
- We must all appear before the judgment seat of Christ, that each one may receive the things done in the body, according to what he has done, good or bad (2 Corinthians 5:10).

May I suggest that there's much more to the afterlife than what NDEs are telling us? There's a vitally important truth that's being overlooked—and even many Christians have overlooked it. Let's see what the Bible has to say about the afterlife.

Two resurrections

This may come as a surprise, but Scripture actually speaks not of one resurrection at the end of the age, but of *two*. That's right, there are two resurrections—two vastly different resurrections. In fact, they are resurrections of people headed in opposite directions, if you can conceive of such a thing. Jesus Himself described these two totally different resurrections. "The hour is coming," He said, "in which all who are in the graves will hear His voice and come forth—those who have done good, to the resurrection of life, and those who have done evil, to the resurrection of condemnation" (John 5:28, 29). So it makes all the difference in the world which resurrection we experience.

Let's look at what John's statement tells us about the first resurrection. First, it's a spectacular event. Paul describes it in 1 Thessalonians:

> The Lord Himself will descend from heaven with a shout, with the voice of an archangel, and with the trumpet of God. And the dead in Christ will rise first. Then we who are alive and remain shall be caught up together with them in the clouds to meet the Lord in the air. And thus we shall always be with the Lord (4:16, 17).

"The dead in Christ will rise first." This is the first resurrection. It takes place at Jesus' second coming. The Bible tells us that Jesus is going to descend from heaven one day—the same Jesus who ministered in Galilee two thousand years ago. Jesus' return is not some mystical event. A very real Jesus will return. The same Jesus who ascended to heaven in a glorious, immortal body will return gloriously (Acts 1:9–11; Matthew 16:27). His coming will be visible. Every eye will see Him come (Matthew 24:30; Revelation 1:7). His coming will be an audible coming, not a silent event. Not only will every eye see Him come, but every ear will hear His coming too (Matthew 24:31; 1 Thessalonians 4:16, 17). "Our God shall come, and shall not keep silent; a fire shall devour before Him, and it shall be very tempestuous all around Him" (Psalm 50:3).

At that time, those who have died in Jesus, those who have developed a relationship with Him, will awaken to a glorious eternity with Him. That trumpet of God pierces down into the tomb, and the same Creator who fashioned life on this planet in the beginning goes to work again, turning skeletons into living human beings, recreating minds and remolding personalities. And then the resurrected join those believers who are still living, and, together with Jesus, they all ascend to heaven in their glorious, immortal bodies.

That incredible journey begins, for all believers, living or dead, with a dramatic transformation at the return of our Lord. Paul describes exactly what will happen to all those who are faithful to Jesus: "We will not all sleep, but we will all be changed—in a flash, in the twinkling of an eye, at the last trumpet. For the trumpet will sound, the dead will be raised imperishable, and we will be changed" (1 Corinthians 15:51, 52, NIV).

Paul tells us it is at this time that believers are given immortality. This is when death is swallowed up in victory. This is when those who are in Jesus receive perfect new bodies, new hearts, and new minds. No sickness, no weakness, no decay will ever touch us again.

In the book of Philippians, Paul further explains what those who eagerly wait for their Savior, those whose citizenship is in heaven, will experience. He says that Jesus Christ "will transform our lowly body that it may be conformed to His glorious body" (Philippians 3:21).

Believers are going to have very real lives with Jesus in very real bodies—glorious bodies. The Bible doesn't describe a mystical, ethereal journey through a long passageway to the "other side" to be embraced there by a being of light. It reveals the return of a very real Jesus. There is a real resurrection. We receive new, immortal bodies and ascend to heaven with our Lord. This is what happens in the first resurrection, the resurrection to eternal life.

But Paul is also very clear about the second resurrection. It takes place after the millennium—the thousand years during which the righteous are in heaven with Jesus. The second resurrection is called a resurrection of condemnation because that's when all the wicked must face God's judgment. Revelation 20 tells us about this resurrection:

> (The rest of the dead did not come to life until the thousand years were ended.). . . The sea gave up the dead that were in it, and death and Hades gave up the dead that were in them, and each person was judged according to what they had done. . . . Anyone whose name was not found written in the book of life was thrown into the lake of fire (Revelation 20:5, 13, 15, NIV).

This is earth's final tragedy. It's an awakening, but not one that ends in eternal life. It's a rising from sleep that leads only to eternal death. It is difficult for us to imagine the sense of loss of those who look at God in all His glory and realize that they will never, never live with Him in heaven. They will miss out on eternity. What inexpressible anguish that thought must bring. No wonder Scripture describes it as a time when there will be weeping and gnashing of teeth.

Two resurrections. Two destinies. Two vastly different eternities.

But here's the important point: we can avoid the second resurrection. No one has to end up in that lake of fire. No one has to experience eternal annihilation.

It's avoidable because of what God has done. The Father isn't just some indifferent judge sitting on his throne and willy-nilly sending this person to one fate and that person to another. He doesn't arbitrarily determine human destinies. No, the Father is very active in trying to rescue us. Look at His appeal in Ezekiel. This is God Himself speaking through the prophet:

> "Therefore, . . . I will judge each of you according to your own ways, declares the Sovereign LORD. Repent! Turn away from all your offenses; then sin will not be your downfall. Rid yourselves of all the offenses you have committed, and get a new heart and a new spirit. Why will you die . . . ? For I take no pleasure in the death of anyone, declares the Sovereign LORD. Repent and live!" (Ezekiel 18:30–32, NIV).

The two resurrections send human beings off in opposite directions. But God says, "No one has to die. Why do you choose to die? Repent and live!"

If we take responsibility for our offenses, if we receive the pardon that Jesus offers because of the cross, if we repent, then we can be assured of being in the first resurrection.

This is the promise that Jesus makes in the book of Revelation: "He who overcomes shall not be hurt by the second death" (Revelation 2:11). We can all escape the finality of the second death. We can all be overcomers. Why? Because, as Scripture tells us, we overcome by the blood of the Lamb. We overcome because Jesus has defeated sin and the power of evil on the cross. We overcome because we find salvation and acceptance through the sacrifice Jesus made. That's how we find eternal life.

The great hope

Do you see that the Bible offers every human being great hope, wonderful hope? This is very different from the vague hope offered by near-death experiences and the religion of the resuscitated. What the Bible promises is more than just existence as a "pool of light." It offers real life with a real God. It says we'll have face-to-face encounters. It pictures paradise with Jesus.

The hope Scripture features isn't value free. No, it takes us seriously as moral beings, as responsible human beings. The hope of Scripture calls us to account. The hope of Scripture asks us to deal honestly with sin. The hope of Scripture goes through the Cross! That's the big difference. That's why Leonid Brezhnev's widow made that sign of the cross on her husband's chest. In the midst of all the pomp and circumstance of the Soviet Empire, she preferred instead the hope offered by a Carpenter from Nazareth. Her gesture flew in the face of the atheistic regime that surrounded her. But she had to cling to something more solid—Someone more solid than anything Communism could offer.

We can have confidence in an afterlife because we can trust Jesus. Through Jesus, we can deal with guilt confidently. We can be assured that the holy God has accepted us. We can have confidence that we'll have an afterlife because we can have confidence we belong to Jesus. That's the kind of hope to cling to. That's a hope that will get us through the roughest times. That's the kind of hope we need.

Let me tell you about a few people who had to face death in the most trying of circumstances.

Real hope for real needs

In August of 1900, during the Boxer uprising in China, Lizzie Atwater, a young mother and missionary, had to face the prospect of a brutal death at the hands of Boxer fanatics who had sworn vengeance on all foreigners. She had to wait in agonizing suspense as the bands of marauders closed in on her compound. As she waited, she clutched a baby to her breast.

But in this time of terror, Lizzie found a way to hope. This is what she wrote to her sister and her family shortly before her death:

I long for a sight of your dear faces, but I fear we shall not meet on earth. . . . I am preparing for the end very quietly and calmly. The Lord is wonderfully near and He will not fail me. I was very restless and excited while there seemed a chance of life, but God has taken away that feeling, and now I just pray for grace to meet the terrible end bravely. The pain will soon be over and, oh, the sweetness of the welcome above![8]

In January of 1956, Roj Youderian was killed while trying to share the gospel with Auca Indians who lived in the jungle in Ecuador. After his body was found, Roj's wife, Barbara, wrote this in her private journal: "God gave me this verse in Psalm 48 two days ago: 'For this God is our God for ever and ever; he will be our guide even unto death' " (Psalm 48:14, KJV).

In November 1964, in the Republic of the Congo, missionary Lois Carlson had to face her husband's death while listening through the static of a shortwave radio. Dr. Paul Carlson's hospital had been overrun by Simba nationalists. Once in a while he could sneak out a brief message on the shortwave. He sent Lois this message: "I know I'm ready to meet my Lord, but my thought for you makes this more difficult. I trust that I might be a witness for Christ."

When they found Dr. Carlson's body at the hospital, there was a New Testament in his jacket pocket. In its pages, the doctor had written the date—it was the day before he was shot—and he'd penned a single word: "Peace."

Peace in the face of the worst of circumstances. Peace in the face of death. People can have peace in the face of death only when they have a profound sense of security, a profound trust in the One who will be with them in the end.

People have peace when they know which resurrection they will experience. They have peace when they know they are going to awaken to see Jesus coming through the clouds, lighting up the sky. They have peace when they know they will be transformed. They have peace when they know they will never again experience heartache and pain and death. They have peace when they know they will spend eternity with Jesus.

Do you have that assurance, or are you just hoping to drift into some vague afterlife? Do you know whose hand will pull you through, or are you just hoping to end up in some pool of light somewhere?

God wants you to live. He has gone to great lengths to enable you to avoid the second resurrection, the resurrection of condemnation. But you have to take a step away from that resurrection—and toward the other. You have to respond to God's call to repent and believe. You have to take your relationship with Him seriously.

Which is it going to be for you: eternal life or a never-ending death?

Which resurrection are you going to choose?

Endnotes

[1] Dannion Brinkley with Paul Perry, *Saved by the Light* (New York: Villard Books, 1994).

[2] Raymond A. Moody Jr., *Life After Life: The Investigation of a Phenomenon—Survival of Bodily Death* (Atlanta: Mockingbird Books, 1975).

[3] Michael Sabom, *Recollections of Death: A Medical Investigation* (New York: Harper & Row, 1981).

[4] Melvin Morse with Paul Perry, *Closer to the Light: Learning From Children's Near Death Experiences* (New York: Villard Books, 1990).

[5] Betty J. Eadie, *Embraced by the Light* (Placerville, CA: Gold Leaf Press, 1992).

[6] Eadie, *Embraced by the Light*, 81.

[7] Kenneth Ring, *Heading Toward Omega: In Search of the Meaning of the Near-Death Experience* (New York: Morrow, 1984).

[8] John R. Hykes, "The Martyr Missionaries in China," *Missionary Review of the World,* new series, 14, no. 2 (February 1901): 89, 90.

Chapter 7

Ready to Meet Jesus

Hundreds of people have been buried on the Mount of Olives, just outside the eastern wall of Old Jerusalem. Why? Many Jews believe that the messiah will appear there when he comes, entering Jerusalem through the Eastern Gate (also known as the Golden Gate) to begin his triumphal reign. Legend also has it that the Shekinah—the Divine Presence—used to enter the city through this gate, and that it will appear there again when the messiah comes.

The Eastern Gate is the only one of the eight main gates in Jerusalem that is sealed. Because the Jews expect their messiah to come through this gate, the Ottoman Turks, when they controlled the city, sealed off the gate with huge stones in A.D. 1541. Then, because the Muslims believed that the Jewish messiah wouldn't set foot in a Muslim cemetery, they added another layer of deterrence by turning the land in front of the gate into a cemetery.

Jesus made His triumphal entry into the city of Jerusalem through the Eastern Gate, and many Christians believe He will return there when He makes His glorious appearance at the Second Coming. That's another reason this hillside is dotted with graves. Apparently, a lot of people want to be first in line for the resurrection!

The hope cherished by those buried there is a hope that people all over the world cling to. All of us want to find some way to transcend death. That's why so many people ask, "Can we really be sure that we'll be part of some glorious resurrection? Can we be sure that we won't be left on the outside?"

For thousands of years, religions have fought—sometimes violently—over Jerusalem. It's a place where people's hopes and dreams for a better future are closely linked to their history. The ancient sites there still speak to people of a past glory and a better tomorrow. Many believe this city will occupy the spotlight when the Messiah returns in glory. They expect Him to set up His kingdom here on earth. They expect Him to usher in a millennium of peace. They expect that Jerusalem will once again become a place where God's people can find safety. But they also expect that before this happens, the antichrist will enter a Jewish temple that has been built on the temple mount in Jerusalem.

Many people are confused about what the Bible actually teaches regarding the end time. Consequently, they've misunderstood what the second coming of Jesus Christ is all about. Because they're focusing on the wrong place and the wrong issue, they may very well misunderstand where the final battle will be fought and what it's all about.

Let me point you to one of the clearest pictures Jesus has given us of what His return will look like. Matthew records Him as saying that

> "the sign of the Son of Man will appear in heaven, and then all the tribes of the earth will mourn, and they will see the Son of Man coming on the clouds of heaven with power and great glory. And He will send His angels with a great sound of a trumpet, and they will gather together His elect from the four winds, from one end of heaven to the other" (Matthew 24:30, 31).

These verses portray the Second Coming. It's a glorious event. It's an event that will be *the* turning point in history. Among other things, it will divide humanity into two parts—those who mourn, and those who are gathered together and join Jesus. The parable of the wheat and the tares concludes with a verbal picture of this division. When the hired help tell their boss that someone has planted weeds in his wheat fields, he says, "Let both grow together until the harvest, and at the time of harvest I will say to the reapers, 'First gather together the tares and bind them in bundles to burn them, but gather the wheat into my barn' " (Matthew 13:30).

What this parable means is pretty clear. When the righteous are gathered to Jesus, the unsaved people of this world will be consumed with the brightness of His coming (2 Thessalonians 1:7–12; Hebrews 12:29).

Here's another picture of the end of history. Jesus explained,

> "When the Son of Man comes in His glory, and all the holy angels with Him, then He will sit on the throne of His glory. All the nations will be gathered before Him, and He will separate them one from another, as a shepherd divides his sheep from the goats" (Matthew 25:31, 32).

This is another picture of judgment being rendered at Jesus' coming. The "sheep"—people who have given themselves to Jesus—are welcomed into the kingdom. But the "goats"—people who have chosen to reject God and the life He offers—end up in the lake of fire, where they're completely consumed, and gone from the universe forever. And every human being chooses either to be a sheep or a goat.

The second coming of Jesus Christ gives a whole new meaning to the term *public event*. Every human being alive at the time of Jesus' glorious appearing in the heavens will witness His coming. "The Son of Man will come in the glory of His Father with His angels, and then He will reward each according to his works" (Matthew 16:27). You can imagine what a glorious event that will be! John the revelator tells us that "He is coming with clouds, *and every eye will see Him*" (Revelation 1:7; emphasis added).

As unexpected as a thief

There's another aspect to the Second Coming—another important truth regarding Jesus' return. While He will come gloriously as Lord of lords and King of kings, for many people, His coming will be as unexpected as that of a thief in the night. Jesus warned,

> "Watch therefore, for you do not know what hour your Lord is coming. But know this, that if the master of the house had known what hour the thief would come, he would have watched and not allowed his house to be broken into. Therefore you also be ready, for the Son of Man is coming at an hour you do not expect" (Matthew 24:42–44).

Peter also compares Jesus' coming to that of a thief: "The day of the Lord will come as a thief in the night" (2 Peter 3:10). Many people have misunderstood this matter of Jesus' coming as being like that of a thief. Notice carefully what the text says. Jesus' coming as a "thief in the night" doesn't mean He's coming and going secretly. No, He comes suddenly, unexpectedly. But when He comes, the "heavens . . . pass away with a great noise, and the elements . . . melt with fervent heat" (verse 10). That hardly sounds as though He's trying to keep His coming a secret!

What does Peter mean by "a thief in the night"? Is Jesus going to sneak up on the planet? If this event is so glorious, if heaven and earth are transformed, why is the coming Jesus pictured as a thief?

Jesus Himself has given us a clue. He shows us that this thief imagery doesn't relate to the manner of His return, but its timing. Like a thief, He will come suddenly, at a time when most people aren't expecting Him.

In Matthew 25, Jesus tells a parable about His return. Ten young women are waiting excitedly to be the guests of a bridegroom at an evening wedding. While they know the bridegroom is coming, they don't know exactly when. But never mind—it will be a joyous event!

Then the bridegroom is delayed, and while the young women wait, they fall asleep. In telling the parable, Jesus says five of the women are wise and five are foolish. However, it isn't staying awake that separates the wise from the foolish. When the bridegroom's arrival at the wedding is delayed, they *all* grow weary and fall asleep.

In what way do the women differ? Five of the women have brought enough oil to keep their lamps lit for longer than they had expected they'd need to. The other five have been careless. They haven't prepared for the unexpected, so they run out of oil and have to go looking for some more. The bridegroom arrives while they're away. He invites the five wise women to witness the wedding. But the five careless women miss it altogether: "While they went to buy, the bridegroom came, and those who were ready went in with him to the wedding; and the door was shut" (Matthew 25:10).

"The door was shut." This powerful image should motivate us to be ready for the return of our Lord despite delays, despite our not knowing when to expect Him. It tells us that Jesus' second coming is a decisive event. Now is the time to prepare. When He returns, that opportunity has come and gone, and eternity is at hand.

How can we be sure that we won't be surprised by Jesus' second coming? How should we prepare for it? To find some solid answers, let's examine Jesus' return and the kingdom He subsequently sets up. We're going to look at one fact in particular—the most important thing we must know to be ready for this great event. Jesus' second coming is the biggest turning point in human history. It's the point in time when the world stops business as usual. When Jesus comes, the destiny of every human being who has ever lived will have been decided.

Notice again Jesus' words as recorded in the book of Matthew: "The Son of Man is going to come in his Father's glory with his angels, and then he will reward each person according to what he has done" (Matthew 16:27, NIV). Jesus returns, and what happens? Each person—every one of us—faces his or her reward. To God, each person's life has been an open book. Now, it's a book that has reached its climax. A verdict is rendered. We know the outcome.

Jesus makes His final appeal to humanity in the last chapter of Revelation, the Bible's last book. There He declares that when He returns, the fate of all humanity is already settled. Every person has made his or her final, irrevocable choice for or against Jesus. Note the solemn declaration made then:

> "He who is unjust, let him be unjust still; he who is filthy, let him be filthy still; he who is righteous, let him be righteous still; he who is holy, let him be holy still."
>
> "And behold, I am coming quickly, and My reward is with Me, to give to every one according to his work" (Revelation 22:11, 12).

If, when Jesus comes, all human beings will receive either eternal life or eternal death, the judgment that determines who will be acquitted and who will be condemned must have already taken place.

Now, the good news is that no one needs to be afraid of that final judgment. The Bible says that all those who place their faith in Jesus have passed out of judgment and into life. He promises that in the judgment He will justify all those who accept Him as Savior. Nevertheless, there will be a final judgment. It will take place in earth's last days, at the end of history. And eternal destinies will be decided.

Misunderstanding end-time events

Many people today, however, give us a different picture of the end of this age. They interpret Old Testament prophecies in a way that contradicts the Bible's picture of the Second Coming. They make it something less than the end. It isn't quite the real judgment. Here's what this popular but mistaken end-time scenario pictures.

To begin with, it divides Jesus' return into two parts. First, there's the secret rapture. Believers disappear. The lost are left behind. This is followed by a seven-year period of tribulation. According to this view, that's when the antichrist rises. At the end of those seven years, Jesus returns to earth again. He lands in Jerusalem and establishes a kingdom on earth. At that point, the millennium begins—the millennium of peace—and all the righteous flock to Jerusalem, while the rest of humankind remains outside. Jerusalem becomes the place from which God's light shines out, enlightening the world. Jesus' followers go out on special millennial missionary ventures, and they manage to win over some of those who hadn't, to that point, given their allegiance to the Messiah. A version of this last-day scenario says that when the antichrist manifests himself during the Tribulation, 144,000 converted Jews preach the gospel to those who haven't been raptured, and many people accept Jesus.

These are widely accepted pictures of the end times. Where do these ideas come from? They grow out of Old Testament prophecies that were given to the nation of Israel—prophecies like the one in Isaiah in which God says, "I will set a sign among them; and those among them who escape I will send to the nations, . . . to the coastlands afar off who have not heard My fame nor seen My glory. And they shall declare My glory among the Gentiles" (Isaiah 66:19). This was God's hope for Israel. He wanted that nation to become a light to the Gentiles.

The leaders of Israel sabotaged that plan. Pharisees and Sadducees plotted to destroy the very Messiah for whom they'd been waiting such a long time. After Jesus' crucifixion, the Jewish people as a religious and political entity could no longer fulfill God's purposes. Jesus mourned what this meant would happen to those who had been His chosen people: "O Jerusalem, Jerusalem, the one who kills the prophets and stones those who are sent to her!" He said, "How often I wanted to gather your children together as a hen gathers her chicks under her wings but you were not willing. See! Your house is left to you desolate" (Matthew 23:37, 38). When the Roman army sacked Jerusalem in A.D. 70, the temple was destroyed as Jesus had predicted.

The writers of the New Testament make it very clear that the promises once made to Israel now apply to the Christian followers of the Messiah. Although individual Jews would continue to accept the gospel and be saved, never again would God work exclusively through the nation of Israel. According to Paul, now it's those who accept Jesus as the Messiah who are the true "seed of Abraham" (Galatians 3:29).

The followers of the Messiah would ultimately declare God's glory among the Gentiles. Jesus prophesied that His disciples would take the gospel to every nation and people. That task will be completed before His second coming.

In the book of Matthew, Jesus listed some of the signs that are to precede His return. He foretold international conflict, famines, pestilences, earthquakes, and increasing crime and immorality as well as a host of other signs. Then He listed the final sign that would be visible before His return: "This gospel of the kingdom will be preached in all the world as a witness to all the nations, and then the end will come" (Matthew 24:14).

The gospel is preached everywhere, and then the end comes. And, yes, the second coming of Jesus is the end of history. Eternal destinies must be decided before that event takes place.

It has become very common these days for Christians to imagine that the Second Coming isn't the end of this age. They imagine that Jesus' return ushers in a millennium during which thousands who live on earth will get another opportunity to make a decision for Him.

However, while we may not understand every little detail of end-time events, the Bible *does* give us the basic picture. We need to be very careful about misunderstanding that basic picture of when history actually does come to an end.

Preparing now for His return

Having more people accept Jesus as Lord after His return may seem to be what God would want, but in reality it is counterproductive and, in fact, dangerous. Here's why. Remember that for many people, Jesus' return in all His divine glory will be as much of a shock as would the invasion of their homes by thieves in the night. They won't be ready for it.

Why?

That's an important question. The parables of Jesus give us a striking answer.

Remember the five careless young women? They were waiting for the bridegroom to appear, but they hadn't bothered to get enough oil for their lamps to get through difficulties that might arise.

Jesus also told a parable about three servants whose master left on a long trip. Before leaving, he gave each of the three some money that they were to invest while he was gone. Two of them invested wisely and made a profit while their boss was away. The third, who didn't trust the boss's decency and fairness, just buried the money he'd been given. He chose to go with what he thought was the safe and easy thing to do. But his boss wasn't about to keep someone on his payroll who had proved to be both lazy and disloyal.

And in a third parable, Jesus told of a father who asked his two sons to work in the family's vineyard. The older son said, "I won't go!" But then he regretted his rash response and went to work pruning the grapevines. The younger son smiled at his dad and said, "Yes, sir; I'll go." However, tending the vineyard wasn't high on his list of priorities, and he ended up doing his own thing.

Through these parables, Jesus shows us why people aren't ready for His second advent, why they're shocked by His return, why His coming is as unexpected as that of a thief in the night.

What do we see? Jesus' parables don't picture individuals who are shaking their fists at God. They aren't actively resisting Him. But they won't allow Him to persuade them to serve Him fully. Yes, they sort of recognize that He is the Master. Yes, they sort of recognize their obligations. But they haven't made up their minds to follow Him wholeheartedly. That's why people aren't ready. That's why the Second Coming is such a shock.

In a very few words, the writer of Hebrews gives us a picture of the difference between the saved and the lost. "We are not of those," he says, "who shrink back and are destroyed, but of those who believe and are saved" (Hebrews 10:39, NIV). Those who aren't quite willing to believe that God has their best interests in mind aren't willing to commit themselves entirely to Him. So they shrink away from the appeals of His Spirit.

God gives us evidence that He is worthy of our trust. He doesn't ask us to leap in the dark without any evidence that He'll provide a safe place to land. However, when we've seen the evidence, we need to make a decision. We have to make up our minds. But so many procrastinate. It seems to be part of human nature to postpone making commitments.

Unfortunately, not making up our minds can become a habit. It's a habit that some end-time scenarios actually reinforce. The pictures of Jesus' return that some people promote actually encourage people to put off making that vital decision. Why decide now if you can do it after the Second Coming? You'll have plenty of time to make that hard choice during the millennium of peace on earth. It'll be easy for you to make up your mind when Jesus has returned in a blaze of glory and has set up His headquarters in Jerusalem.

The popular view

In the popular view of the end times, believers are raptured into heaven before the Tribulation. In effect, then, those who hold this position are telling us, "Don't worry about the Tribulation. You won't have to go through that trial." Compare that with the model that stands behind the Tribulation that Revelation pictures—the ten plagues that so troubled the Egyptians. It's true that most of those plagues didn't touch Israel; they fell only on the Egyptians. But Israel did suffer the first three too. And remember that the seven last plagues fall on earth before Jesus' glorious return. The exodus of the church from the earth will take place after the plagues of the last days, just as the exodus of Israel from Egypt took place after the plagues of Moses' day.

So, yes, we need to be ready for the Tribulation. We need to make decisions today that will enable us to stand fast tomorrow. I believe in a God who can take us through any trial. He hasn't promised to take us out of all our trials, but He has promised to stand with us—just as He stood with Shadrach, Meshach, and Abednego in the fiery furnace; just as He stood with Daniel in the lions' den; just as He stood with Paul in prison.

The biblical pattern pictures deliverance coming to those who keep their faith in God in the midst of trial. So we need to make sure our faith is resting upon a strong foundation. We need to make up our minds today. We need to make the right commitment before the Tribulation starts. If we haven't made up our minds by then, it will be too late.

The reason people don't commit usually isn't that they need more information. It isn't that they can't understand what God is asking them to do. It's really that they can't make up their minds. They can't, or won't, make the hard decision to give up their will and follow God's will for them instead. Ultimately, the battle over Jerusalem is a battle of wills.

Accepting Jesus as Lord is a matter of making a decision. We must battle the urge to indulge our own wills. God requires our allegiance. Accepting Jesus as our Savior leads us to acknowledge Him as our Lord. Then our strongest desire will be to do His will. Like Jesus in Gethsemane, we'll cry out from the depths of our being, "Not as I will, but as You will" (Matthew 26:39). We'll long to live obedient, godly lives because we are convinced that the way He calls us to live is really the best way to live.

It's vitally important for us to make up our minds now about where we stand. To have a choice, we must make the choice before history ends—before Jesus comes. That's why God gives people invitations like the one recorded in the book of Revelation. There the apostle John has written about the Jesus who will return to earth. He's written about the end of history. Then he makes this invitation: "The Spirit and the bride say, 'Come!' And let him who hears say, 'Come!' And let him who thirsts come. And whoever desires, let him take the water of life freely" (Revelation 22:17).

The Spirit of Jesus Christ invites us to come. Whoever desires, whoever wants to, can come and receive the Water of Life. It's up to us. It's a matter of choice. And it's time for us to make up our minds.

Have you been putting off that decision? Have you imagined that there will always be another day, another chance? Is there something standing between you and Jesus' kingdom? Have you allowed something to block you from making life's most important commitment? Something at work, or something at home? Maybe a secret you've never dared share with anyone?

Now is the time for you to make up your mind. Now is the time to decide—now, before indecision becomes a habit. Now is the time to choose which kingdom you are going to belong to for eternity. It's your choice. It's your life. Put yourself in God's hands. This could be the moment that decides your eternal destiny.

Will the Temple Be Rebuilt?

Many people believe that the Temple Mount in Old Jerusalem will catapult the earth into its final days. They believe the end time will begin there, where a Muslim shrine—the Dome of the Rock—now stands, where two successive Jewish temples once stood, and where many Jews believe a third temple will be built in the future. Numerous Christians are sure that God's final invasion of history turns on the rebuilding of that temple.

Does it? Is this a vital biblical truth or a dangerous misconception? Will Israel's temple be rebuilt just before the return of our Lord? To fully understand the answers to these questions we must first know the history of the temple.

The Bible indicates that the first temple was built around 957 B.C. by King Solomon. His temple replaced the portable sanctuary that the Israelites had built, following God's instruction, to provide a place for worship as they journeyed from Egypt to Canaan. Sheshonk I, pharaoh of Egypt, ransacked this temple a few decades later. In 835 B.C., Jehoash, who was in only the second year of his reign as king of Judah, invested considerable sums in its reconstruction. Sennacherib, king of Assyria, stripped the temple of valuables in about 700 B.C., and the Babylonians destroyed it completely in 586 B.C.

According to the book of Ezra, construction of the second temple was authorized by Cyrus the Great. The Jews began to work on that temple in 538 B.C., and it was completed twenty-three years later.

though that temple wasn't as imposing as its predecessor or as richly furnished, it still dominated the skyline of Jerusalem. Enlarged and remodeled by Herod the Great—the Herod who was ruling when Jesus was born—this second temple was destroyed by the Romans in A.D. 70.

The Temple Mount Center

The Temple Mount Center is located in the Jewish Quarter of the Old City of Jerusalem. Its Web site declares that "its purpose is to arouse the hearts of the people and awaken the will and the desire to build the . . . Holy Third Temple—speedily in our days." Its supporters believe that nothing "stands in the way of a determined will" and that the third temple will be built on the Temple Mount.

For years, Rabbi Tsvi Rogin, a Hasidic Jew who was the director of the Temple Mount Center, followed a rigid daily routine. He rose at 5:00 A.M., took a ritual bath to purify himself, and arrived at the entrance to the Temple Mount by 7:20 A.M. so he would be first in line for entry. Israeli police officers would search him carefully for weapons and then allow him onto the grounds, but only with an escort—an Israeli officer wearing a bulletproof vest walked on one side of him, and a Muslim official holding a two-way radio walked on the other side. If the rabbi stopped for a moment, both of his guards would become anxious and urge him to keep moving. They were trying to prevent, at all costs, Rogin's lips from moving in prayer. To allow him to pray in this particular spot would be like dropping a burning match into a powder keg. Rogin has been expelled from the Temple Mount for merely appearing to pray.

Tsvi Rogin came day after day. He came to breathe the air on the Temple Mount. He was still obsessed with the idea that the third Jewish temple will be rebuilt there, and he was preparing for that glorious day—though he wouldn't say what his preparing involved. He apparently believed that the mosques there would somehow just disappear.

Others haven't been content only to visit the Temple Mount and to hope. Jewish extremists have launched several plots to destroy the mosques. Each time, Israeli authorities have managed to foil the attempts, so no explosions have shattered the Dome of the Rock. But many Muslims fear that eventually a plot may succeed.

This is the place where, for hundreds of years, Hebrew priests offered sacrifices. This is the place where Solomon's glorious temple stood. This is the place where incense rose from the altar before the Most Holy Place to the God of heaven.

Muslims dismiss the Jewish claims, making their own instead. They believe this to be the place from which Muhammad ascended to heaven. The Dome of the Rock covers the site and commemorates that supposed event. The al-Aqsa Mosque stands on the Temple Mount too. Its minarets broadcast Muslim calls to prayer throughout the day; so Jewish worship there would be considered a virtual act of war.

Muslims vehemently dispute the Jewish claims to this piece of ground, which members of both religions consider sacred. One young Palestinian woman, angry that Jews would venture to visit the Temple Mount, exclaimed, "We are Muslims. Allah said that the mosque is only for Muslims. Why are they coming here? What temple? Where?" She quickly dismissed all assertions that two temples were built on the mount and destroyed in biblical times.

Christians and the Temple Mount

Now, many Christians are looking at the Temple Mount with increasing interest. They see it as a place where prophecy will be fulfilled, a place where the time of the end will get a jump-start. Why? A particular mode of prophetic interpretation has become very popular in the last few decades. It has become the dominant view among many conservative Christians. The nation of Israel, they believe, will play a role in the dramatic conclusion of earth's history.

So, should we be looking to Jerusalem? Will the temple be rebuilt? Is that what the Bible predicts? Let's take a careful look at the evidence.

Here's a prophecy that those who hold this view often cite:

> Now it shall come to pass in the latter days that the mountain of the LORD's house shall be established on the top of the mountains, and shall be exalted above the hills; and all nations shall flow to it. Many people shall come and say, "Come, and let us go up to the mountain of the LORD, to the house of the God of Jacob; He will teach us His ways, and we shall walk in His paths." For out of Zion shall go forth the law, and the word of the LORD from Jerusalem (Isaiah 2:2, 3).

So, Isaiah says that "in the latter days," people from all over the world will come to "the mountain of the LORD's house" in Jerusalem. They will come to learn about God's ways. They will come to walk in God's paths.

Isaiah is picturing a spiritual renaissance that centers in Jerusalem, in God's house. And this prophecy is just one of many that foretells a glorious future for Israel. God did indeed want His chosen people to become the light of the world. He wanted to bless all nations through Israel.

When we look at the evidence, we find, unfortunately, that the people of Israel often failed Him. The Old Testament tells the story of their apostasies and of God's efforts to win them back. In fact, God was still calling to them after Jerusalem was destroyed and its inhabitants led off to exile in Babylon. God promised that if they would just come back to Him, He would still make them a great nation. Note this vision of Israel restored that Ezekiel recorded: "I will make a covenant of peace with them, and it shall be an everlasting covenant with them; I will establish them and multiply them, and I will set My sanctuary in their midst forevermore" (Ezekiel 37:26).

God wanted to establish His sanctuary in Jerusalem as a place of light, a place of revelation, so, after decades of exile, the prophets inspired some faithful Jews to return to Jerusalem and rebuild temple. There was still hope for them. They could still become the light of the world.

Hundreds of years later, the people of Israel did have their date with destiny. They had a rendezvous with the Messiah. Jesus was born among them—actually, became one of them. And He began to proclaim that the kingdom of heaven had come, that it was present among the Jews.

But here is one of the great tragedies of history. Many members of the nation that had been waiting so long for the Messiah—waiting generation after generation—missed the message, missed the Man, and missed the kingdom. They thought the Messiah would come as a mighty conqueror to defeat their national enemies and restore Israel's greatness. They didn't understand that the Messiah was to come twice: first as a Suffering Servant who would usher in the kingdom of grace, and then as a triumphant King who would establish the kingdom of glory.

God came down to earth. He unleashed grace and peace on this planet. But many of the Jews didn't see what was happening—didn't welcome the kingdom of heaven. Lepers were healed, blind eyes opened, deaf ears unstopped, demoniacs delivered, and the oppressed freed. But many of the Jews were too tied to their city on earth. They were focused on their holy temple in Zion. They were so obsessed with the presence of God in their temple that they missed His presence in the person of Jesus Christ. They thought Jesus was a threat to their traditions. So, the Jewish leaders who controlled Israel conspired against Him. They tried to get rid of Him, and they succeeded—temporarily.

Israel's destiny

So, what became of the nation of Israel? What happened to that holy temple that God wanted to make the center of worship on the earth?

Jesus knew what would happen to both the nation and the

ple. When some of His followers commented on the beauty of
the temple, He replied, "These things which you see—the days will
come in which not one stone shall be left upon another that shall not
be thrown down" (Luke 21:6). Saddened by the prospect, He also
said, "See! Your house is left to you desolate" (Matthew 23:38).

Those who heard Jesus were shocked. God's holy temple would
be destroyed? That was inconceivable! But that's exactly what happened. The spiritual desolation came first. When Jesus died on the
cross, the veil that separated the temple's Holy Place from its Most
Holy Place was split in two, and the presence of God departed, never
to return. And nearly forty years later, the Roman general Titus
sacked Jerusalem and leveled the temple.

But Jesus knew all those wonderful promises about a restored
Israel and the sanctuary that was supposed to be established forever.
How did He know they wouldn't be fulfilled, that, instead, the Jews
would be scattered and their temple destroyed?

He knew it because the Pharisees and Sadducees and the scribes
and the elders were plotting His death. They were determined to
destroy the One who could have fulfilled their hopes. They passion-
ately rejected the Messiah, the core of their identity as a nation.

That's why Jesus knew that Israel's days as the light of the world
were numbered. The leaders of the Jews were consumed with a temple that had become an empty shell. All its ceremonies had pointed
forward to the sacrificial death of the Messiah, but the vast majority
of the Jewish leaders misunderstood the meaning of those sacrifices.
The keepers of the temple did their best to shut out the true Sacrifice
when He finally came, so the temple was reduced to rubble.

What are we to think, then, of those Old Testament prophecies
and the end times? Have all the ancient hopes for Israel simply been
wiped away? Have all the promises of a glorious future been canceled?

No, they haven't. In Romans 9–11, Paul takes pains to tell us just
what happened to God's plan. He reminds his Roman readers that
his fellow Jews are the ones to whom God originally gave His cove-

nant, His law, and His promises. And then he says, "They are not all Israel who are of Israel" (Romans 9:6).

What does that mean? Paul explains a few verses later: "Those who are the children of the flesh, these are not the children of God; but *the children of the promise are counted as the seed*" (verse 8; emphasis added). Paul says it isn't genealogy that gives people a place among the chosen. It's the acceptance of God's promise. It's a matter of faith. That's the way it was for Abraham, the original Jewish patriarch. That's the way it is for everyone else.

In Galatians, Paul makes the content of that faith clear: "If you belong to Christ, then you are Abraham's seed, and heirs according to the promise" (Galatians 3:29, NIV). Placing your faith in Jesus the Messiah makes you a son of Abraham. It makes you an heir of His legacy. After all, Jesus was the culmination of Hebrew history. It all came together in Him. He was the true dwelling of God on earth. He was the true sacrifice. He was the true fulfillment of the law. So all the blessings promised to Israel now belong to the followers of the Messiah—whoever they might be, Jew or Gentile. The commission God gave Israel to light up the world is now the responsibility of the followers of Jesus, the Messiah.

Paul tells us that anyone who believes can be grafted into the original vine, the Hebrew vine that God watered and nurtured for so long. People of all backgrounds, all races, and all nationalities can become part of the chosen—part of God's family.

God's plan for Israel has now become God's plan for believers—for all who place their faith in Him. Do you realize what that means? God's prophecies about Israel now become prophecies about believers. Remember that *all* God's promises are *Yes* in Jesus. They are given to His followers, the seed of Abraham, no matter what their racial background is.

But what do we find today? We find many Christians focused on the nation of Israel because they think it will play a key role in end-time events.

Looking in the wrong place

All those who have focused their eyes on Israel are looking in the wrong place. They're looking for a kingdom to be built on earth when we need to be looking for a kingdom delivered from heaven. They're focusing on political events instead of spiritual events. They're paying more attention to the work of the antichrist on earth than on the ministry of the genuine Christ in heaven. And above all, their attention is centered on an earthly temple instead of a heavenly temple.

That's right, a heavenly temple. Do you realize that the New Testament directs our attention toward a heavenly temple as part of the new covenant of faith and grace?

Let's take a look at the book of Hebrews. This remarkable document was written for Jews. It shows how their religious practices find their ultimate fulfillment in Jesus. It shows that the Jewish temple is really all about Jesus—that all the sacrifices in the temple rituals pointed to Jesus' sacrifice on Calvary; that His death makes all those sacrifices meaningful. It shows that Jesus is the ultimate High Priest. And it shows that Jesus is the Mediator of a new covenant, a better covenant—one that provides for us an eternal inheritance.

Here's how the author sums up the primary truth God meant the Jewish temple to teach:

> Now this is the main point of the things we are saying:
> We have such a High Priest, who is seated at the right hand
> of the throne of the Majesty in the heavens, a Minister of
> the sanctuary and of the true tabernacle which the Lord
> erected, and not man (Hebrews 8:1, 2).

Here are the vital truths we can learn from the book of Hebrews: The true tabernacle is in heaven. Everything that happened in the earthly sanctuary pointed forward to Jesus' life, death, resurrection, and ministry as our Intercessor and High Priest in the heavenly sanctuary.

The earthly sanctuary was not an end in itself. God told M that the earthly sanctuary should be built "according to the patte which was shown you on the mountain" (Exodus 25:40). In earth last days, we shouldn't focus our attention upon a Jewish high priest ministering in a rebuilt temple in Jerusalem. Rather, we should focus it upon Jesus, our great High Priest in the temple in heaven.

The apostle Paul continues his discussion of Jesus' high-priestly ministry: "Christ came as High Priest of the good things to come, with the greater and more perfect tabernacle not made with hands, that is, not of this creation" (Hebrews 9:11).

The author of Hebrews reveals that the furnishings of the temple on earth are copies of things that are in heaven. In fact, the temple itself is a copy of the true temple in heaven. Notice what Hebrews 9:24 says, "Christ has not entered the holy places made with hands, *which are copies of the true,* but into heaven itself, now to appear in the presence of God for us" (emphasis added).

Jesus, the ultimate High Priest, is actually appearing before God on our behalf in a heavenly sanctuary, the heavenly temple. That is where the New Testament places Him. That is where the New Testament directs our hope.

Notice this rousing call: "Having boldness to enter the Holiest by the blood of Jesus, . . . let us draw near with a true heart in full assurance of faith" (Hebrews 10:19, 22). We can approach the very throne of God *boldly*! We can have full assurance in our faith. Why? Because we have such a wonderful Mediator; because we have such a wonderful High Priest; because we have such a wonderful Advocate in heaven. That's where the New Testament fixes our hope. That's where it centers our attention. It tells us to look there now, and it tells us to look there in the end times.

The book of Revelation is full of images of Jesus in the heavenly temple—a glorious Jesus who walks among the seven lampstands; a glorious Jesus who has spoken to the churches down through the ages and who speaks to us today. Worshipers bow before Him joy-

y in an awesome temple in which lightning flashes and thunder
rs. Angels carrying God's last warning message come flying out
f that temple. Voices from the temple warn about the final dramatic events of earth's history.

Heaven opens up when Jesus comes out in triumph, riding on a
white horse—when He triumphantly leads His angelic armies down
to the earth. The New Testament points us to the sanctuary in
heaven, where our hope can rest secure. It's there that we have a divine Advocate and Friend. It's there that we have a safe place with
God.

We don't have to be afraid of plots involving a temple in Jerusalem. We don't have to worry about Jewish extremists trying to blow
up the Dome of the Rock. We don't have to fret over Arab vows to
take revenge if anyone desecrates their sacred mosque. We don't have
to try to figure out how some rebuilt temple and its sacrifices could
fit into God's end-time plan. We don't have to tremble at the thought
of the antichrist and the coming Tribulation. We shouldn't be focused on what's happening on earth. That's the wrong place to look.
That's the wrong orientation with which to read prophecy. As Paul
says, we should be "looking unto Jesus, the author and finisher of
our faith" (Hebrews 12:2). He is our hope. Our faith must be anchored in heaven's sanctuary, where our great High Priest ministers
for us. We can come "boldly to the throne of grace, that we may obtain mercy and find grace to help in time of need" (Hebrews 4:16).

God's plan isn't about an earthly kingdom. It's about a heavenly
kingdom. God's plan isn't about an earthly temple. It's about a heavenly temple. Many people, in their rush to read political hotspots
into Bible prophecy, have forgotten these basic facts. They try to
make the latest conflict between Israelis and Palestinians a sign of
the end times. But God's plan doesn't depend on territorial conflicts
in Jerusalem. In fact, it's God's plan that is the solution to territorial
conflicts in Jerusalem.

Geography divides. Spirituality unites. God's plan centers on a heavenly temple in which all human beings—whatever their races, whatever their nationalities, whatever their backgrounds—can come boldly before Him. God's plan centers on Jesus as the One who gave Himself up for us all. God's plan centers on the Messiah who can lift us out of our constant quarrels and into His kingdom. God's plan is built from the top down. It flows from the throne of the Almighty all the way down to our problems here on earth.

Yehuda Amichai is widely regarded as the poet laureate of Israel. He told of coming upon two lovers embracing in a Jerusalem street. Aware of the weight of history that hangs over the city, he said with a smile, "Be careful because here, every love can turn into a new religion."[1]

Well, if it really were love that turned into religion, we would have few problems in Jerusalem or anywhere else. Too often it's hate that turns into religion. It's prejudice that turns into religion. It's pride that turns into religion. It's aggression that turns into religion.

We desperately need love to turn into religion. We need the love of a heavenly Father who has a plan for us, a heavenly Father who won't give up on us. We need the love of a God who creates for us a place of safety—the love of a God who assures us that we can come boldly before Him in time of need.

Where is your focus today? Is it on an earthly temple or the heavenly temple? Is it on the antichrist or the real Christ? Is it on what God longs to do for the Jews, or what He longs to do in your own life?

I urge you to fix your hope on the Lord of heaven and earth. I recommend with all my heart Jesus' kingdom of heaven. It's the one place of safety in a world full of hatred and conflict. It's the one place where we can find peace at the feet of our heavenly Father. Your hope can rest secure in heaven. You can be assured that the holy God who is your heavenly Father will welcome you.

I invite you to respond to the call of the apostles who wrote so eloquently in the New Testament. They center our hope on the One who came to live for us and to die for us, on the One who came to conquer death for us and to ascend to heaven for us. They ask us to place our faith in the Mediator of a new covenant, in the High Priest of a better temple. They ask us to fix our gaze on Him, now, tomorrow, and in the end times. He's the same wonderful Savior yesterday, today, and forever. The One who died for you now lives for you, and the One who lives for you is coming again to take you to a better land!

Endnote

[1] Quoted in "The Militant Poet," *Newsweek,* July 23, 2000, archived at the *Daily Beast,* http://bit.ly/NidgXw.

The Trouble With Antichrist

It's not an uncommon sight these days—Israeli soldiers patrolling the streets of Jerusalem. Armored vehicles rolling through the city. Gun-toting young military draftees marching to the Western Wall. At times the ancient Holy City looks as though it's being invaded or under siege. The perennial question is, Who's invading whom? Are the rock-throwing Palestinians trying to take over more Israeli soil, or are the Israelis occupying the homeland of the Palestinians? Jerusalem seems always to be on the verge of a showdown, and the tension there speaks to many people of a final showdown that's on its way. It prefigures a final invasion—by the antichrist himself.

What's the conflict all about? That's the big question when it comes to Christ versus the antichrist.

During the past several decades, Israel has been going through what we might well call a "time of trouble." It's a state of continual unrest. The intifada—the Palestinian uprising—flares up regularly. Israelis, whose weaponry is superior, stifle the protests. But then terrorists strike. Bombs go off in buses or marketplaces. And Israelis crack down on groups like Hamas that claim responsibility. Jerusalem remains a flashpoint, and its citizens seek ways to survive the many perils of their time of trouble.

Jerusalem, of course, is also regarded by many Christians as the place that will be the primary hotspot during the end of time. So much religious history focuses on this city. So many prophecies mention this place. So many Christians believe that a time of trouble—a time of ulation that precedes Jesus' coming—will start here.

What exactly does the Bible say about the Tribulation? Does it show us how to survive it? Does it point to a way through? Let's look for some answers.

One fact comes through pretty clearly: The Tribulation is closely tied to the antichrist. The coming of one is linked to the coming of the other. In Revelation, the antichrist is referred to as "the beast." He makes a dramatic appearance in chapter 13, arising out of the sea. And when he arises, he makes trouble, stimulating the passage of a law that says, "No one may buy or sell except one who has the mark or the name of the beast" (Revelation 13:17). So, the beast exercises coercive power. He even tries to kill all those who will not worship his image.

In Daniel's prophecy, the antichrist is referred to as "the little horn." Daniel says, "I was watching [in vision]; and the same horn was making war against the saints, and prevailing against them" (Daniel 7:21). In Matthew 24, Jesus links deceivers who come saying, "I am the Christ" with a spate of "wars and rumors of wars" (verses 5, 6). And in 2 Thessalonians 2:3, the apostle Paul mentions two events that precede the day of Jesus' coming: "the falling away," and the revealing of "the man of sin."

This man of sin, this "son of perdition," is the antichrist. And "the falling away" refers to a time when people—under pressure, under coercion—fall away from, or lose, their faith. That's the time of trouble. And it's not an accident. It's not something God arbitrarily sends to test people. It's the antichrist—someone who works *against* Jesus—who's responsible for the Tribulation.

Surviving the Tribulation is really a matter of surviving the antichrist. When we understand how to resist him, we'll understand how to make it through the time of trouble he causes.

Remember that this is a spiritual battle. Survival isn't a matter of stockpiling enough canned goods in your basement. It's not a matter of toughening up, of learning how to withstand pain. Surviving this battle is a matter of the state of your spirit, the state of your soul.

Look at this gem from Hebrews. It reveals what will enable us to survive in the coming time of trouble: "Let us run with perseverance the race marked out for us. Let us fix our eyes on Jesus, the author and perfecter of our faith" (Hebrews 12:1, 2, NIV).

How can you make it to the end of the race? How can you learn how to run with perseverance, with endurance? Fix your eyes on Jesus. Center your attention on Him.

That's important enough in normal times, but it will be especially important in the end times. The antichrist wants very badly to deceive us. In fact, he wants to mesmerize us. Notice how Revelation describes the antichrist's activities. John writes, "He performs great signs, so that he even makes fire come down from heaven on the earth in the sight of men. And he deceives those who dwell on the earth by those signs which he was granted to do" (Revelation 13:13, 14).

The antichrist wants to deceive you. He is the representative of Satan, of whom Jesus said, "There is no truth in him. When he speaks a lie, he speaks from his own resources, for he is a liar and the father of it" (John 8:44).

It was Satan who deceived the first human couple, Adam and Eve, in the Garden of Eden. God had warned them not to eat of the forbidden fruit, but Satan told them, "It's OK. Eat some—nothing bad will happen." Satan used deception to lead this couple into disobedience, and he's been deceiving people ever since. Because of this danger, we need to keep our attention focused on Jesus. That's the first essential to surviving the time of trouble.

Who's on center stage?

Is it not ironic that many sincere believers give the antichrist center stage in all kinds of ways? It even happens in the way we look at the Bible. Take the prophecy in Daniel 9, for example. This is a key prophecy that looks to the coming of the Messiah. Daniel 9:25 points forward from the decree to "restore and build Jerusalem" to the time of

Messiah the Prince." Verse 26 says, "Messiah shall be cut off, but not for Himself." This is a prediction of Jesus' death on the cross, of His stand at Calvary, "not for Himself" but for sinful humanity.

Then verse 27 says, "He shall confirm a covenant with many for one week; but in the middle of the week he shall bring an end to sacrifice and offering."

Who confirmed a covenant? Surely this was the Messiah. Just before Jesus' trial and crucifixion, He met with His disciples in the upper room and instituted the Communion service. As He took the wine that represented the blood He was about to shed on Calvary, He said, "This is My blood of the new covenant, which is shed for many for the remission of sins" (Matthew 26:28). Our Redeemer sealed the new covenant with His own blood!

Who, then, brought an end to "sacrifice and offering"? Surely this also points to Jesus. He, and not the antichrist, was the Originator of the covenant. Let's look at the covenant for a bit.

The word *covenant* is used more than three hundred times in the Bible. It appears in thirty-three of the Bible's sixty-six books. The theme of the covenant is God's plan—what He will do to save the people He created. God sets the terms of the covenant. He is the Originator and Author of the covenant. He initiates His covenant for His people. When the theme of God's covenant of grace and salvation is introduced in Genesis, God calls it "the everlasting covenant" (Genesis 9:16) and repeatedly says that He's the one taking the initiative in making the covenant: "I will establish My covenant," "I will make My covenant," and "My covenant will I establish" (Genesis 6:18; 17:2, 21).

God had Jesus' sacrifice on the cross in mind when He established the covenant. Jesus' death was the reality toward which all the sacrifices offered in Old Testament times pointed. After His death, those sacrifices were no longer needed because the real sacrifice—the one that was effectual—had been made. This seems plain enough, yet a very different interpretation has gained popularity in recent years. Many Christians are now applying the line in Daniel's

prophecy that reads "then he shall confirm the covenant with ma̶
for one week" not to the Messiah but to the antichrist! For son̶
reason, they think Daniel's words place the antichrist on center
stage.

In the end time, they tell us, the antichrist is going to make a
peace treaty with the Jews of Israel. They say that's what the words
"he shall confirm a covenant with many" mean. And then, they continue, this evil power will bring an end to "sacrifice and offering" in
the temple. Of course, that means there has to be a temple, and it has
to be functioning. So, those who interpret Daniel in this way tell us
that the Jews will someday build a temple on the Temple Mount in
Jerusalem.

It is my firm belief that the people who accept this interpretation see
the antichrist in scriptural passages where they should be seeing Jesus.
Scripture never says the antichrist confirms a covenant with anyone. That
phrase is almost always applied to the Messiah. And surely all of Daniel
9:24–27 applies to the Messiah, not to the antichrist.

The new covenant

The author of Hebrews writes about a new covenant that Jesus
confirmed with His own blood. It is based on God's word, not on
ours. It is anchored in His promises, not in ours. It is founded on
what He has done, not on what we hope to do. Jesus' sacrificial death
ratified a very special covenant. God put it this way:

> "For this is the covenant that I will make with the house of
> Israel after those days, says the LORD: I will put My laws in
> their mind and write them on their hearts; and I will be
> their God, and they shall be My people" (Hebrews 8:10,
> quoting Jeremiah 31:33).

Through Jesus' grace, He unites us with God, and we become
His people in a very special way. God writes His law in our minds

...d in our hearts. He writes His law in our minds so we know what ...e wants us to do, and He writes it in our hearts so we will love to do what it says. Paul tells us,

> By grace you have been saved through faith, and that not of yourselves; it is the gift of God, not of works, lest anyone should boast. For we are His workmanship, created in Christ Jesus for good works, which God prepared beforehand that we should walk in them (Ephesians 2:8–10).

The New Testament covenant of grace leads to obedience. It causes us to love obedience. It changes us so that we long to fulfill the righteous requirements of the law, as Paul said. Jesus' new covenant offers us forgiveness for the past and a new life in the future—a new life of joyful obedience.

It is this covenant that Satan intends to destroy. Satan the deceiver, Satan the father of lies, wants to deceive us into breaking the covenant with God. He wants us to believe that God's grace isn't able to transform us into obedient Christians. He wants us to believe that sin is so powerful that the blood of Jesus can't give us victory over the sins that beset us. He wants to convince us that grace means we can continue to accommodate our sinful desires and tendencies.

The antichrist wants us to focus on our weakness rather than on Jesus' strength. He wants us to look at how evil we are rather than at how good Jesus is. The antichrist is bent on subverting the victory over sin that Jesus has made possible. He will try to make us believe, just as he did Adam and Eve in the Garden, that obedience doesn't really matter. He will palm off on us his great lie that we are a law unto ourselves and that we needn't give God our absolute obedience.

Revelation tells us the antichrist will be extraordinarily successful in his deception. It says, "He deceives those who dwell on the earth by those signs which he was granted to do" (Revelation 13:14), and it adds that what seems to be the whole world follows this charismatic figure. That's the trouble with the antichrist. That's the danger. God is calling the whole world back to understand the value of obedience, the value of the eternal principles He's laid out for us, and Satan is working for all he's worth to disrupt God's message.

Revelation 14:6–13 is a remarkable passage that pictures three angels flying down to earth to deliver God's final warning messages. That the messengers are pictured as angels conveys the importance of these messages. We're being called to genuine worship. "Fear God," the angels cry, "and worship Him who made heaven and earth." In other words, we need to recover reverence for our Creator.

Then the angels warn us about a false system of worship, a system represented—symbolized—by Babylon. It is Babylon revisited—Babylon, the center of occult worship and idolatry. The angels warn that in the end times these issues will again divide humanity. We'll have to choose between true and false worship. We'll have to choose between worshiping the Creator and Redeemer on one hand and following some dazzling miracle worker on the other. We'll have to choose between obeying God's clear commands and obeying human traditions and dogmas.

Jesus inspires people to reach higher than they are currently reaching—to respond to the law written in their hearts. He inspires them to respond to His love for them by giving Him their obedience. The antichrist opposes eternal moral principles. Scripture calls him "the man of lawlessness." He deceives people into thinking obedience really doesn't matter.

But the people who have come to trust God for their salvation appreciate His holy law. They cherish His Ten Commandments. Look at this picture of God's survivors—His end-time people: "Here is the patience of the saints [believers]; here are those who keep the commandments of God and the faith of Jesus" (Revelation 14:12). These people don't fall for the deceptions of the antichrist. They don't worship the beast; they worship the Creator. They don't ignore the commandments of God; their faith in Jesus leads them to keep those commandments.

The issues in the final conflict of earth's history are larger than the antichrist's occupying of an earthly temple. They involve the great controversy between God and evil, and the matter of whom we will enthrone in the temple of our hearts. These momentous final scenes of earth's history direct our attention to the heavenly sanctuary. They lead us to a deeper commitment of faith in and obedience to Jesus, our heavenly High Priest.

Mere human nature and human efforts won't carry us through the Tribulation. The antichrist and his followers will overcome those who think they can make it through the end time on their own.

How can we survive the Tribulation? We can survive it only if we're strengthened by the love of Jesus—strengthened by the One who gave His life for us. We can survive it only if we allow Him to write His law in our minds and in our hearts.

Stand for a principle, not for a place

Another point about survival: to survive, we must stand for a principle, not for a place. During the time of the prophet Daniel, Nebuchadnezzar—king of Babylon, the most powerful empire on earth at that time—decreed that everyone under his authority was to bow to a huge golden statue that he'd had erected. This statue was a counterfeit—a "correction"—of one he'd seen in a dream God had given him about the future.

The golden head of that statue represented Nebuchadnezzar's kingdom, Babylon. But as rich and powerful as Babylon was, it wouldn't last forever. The dream pictured the chest and arms of the image being made of silver, indicating that another power (the Medes and the Persians) would replace Babylon as the empire to be reckoned with. The dream also pictured other empires to follow and then a time when no single power would control the world, followed, finally, by the return of earth to God's sole sovereignty.

Nebuchadnezzar, however, intended the Babylon he created to last forever. That's why the image he raised on the Plain of Dura was gold from head to foot. And Nebuchadnezzar wanted everyone to endorse his vision of the future. He required everyone in Babylon to come and bow down before this image. "Everyone" included three Hebrew exiles—Shadrach, Meshach, and Abednego. If they wouldn't yield their conscientious convictions and worship the golden image despite God's commands, they would be thrown into a furnace that was heated seven times hotter than it had ever been before. Consequently, those three Hebrews were facing a time of trouble greater than any they had ever faced before.

Those young men had been captured when their beloved Jerusalem was destroyed. They had lost a lot more than their country. The God of heaven had His holy temple in Jerusalem, and that had been destroyed too. Now these young Hebrews were being coerced to compromise their integrity. They faced the choice of either participating in false worship or being executed.

Now that they were in a far-off place, it would have been easy for them to adopt all the gods and beliefs of the Babylonians. They could have made surviving in this new environment their highest priority. That option surely seemed very tempting when they were assembled with thousands of others before the golden statue, and the signal to bow down was sounded. But the three Hebrews didn't bow, and they stood out like sore thumbs.

Nebuchadnezzar was outraged. He threatened to throw the Hebrews into the fiery furnace he had prepared for anyone who disobeyed his decree. That is when these young men showed that they weren't standing on a place—they were standing on a principle. They said,

"Our God whom we serve is able to deliver us from the burning fiery furnace, and He will deliver us from your hand, O king. But if not, let it be known to you, O king, that we do not serve your gods, nor will we worship the gold image which you have set up" (Daniel 3:17, 18).

The three faithful Hebrews weren't raptured before the Tribulation. They weren't delivered from the trial—they were delivered *in* the trial. They believed in an all-powerful God who could deliver. He could deliver people who lived in Jerusalem. And He could deliver people who lived in Babylon. It was a matter of principle that they worship Him only. They were going to remain true to Him even if it meant dying in a blazing furnace.

This story is justly famous. You remember how it goes. The three Hebrews are cast into the fire, God walks with them in the flames, and they emerge unscathed. In the greatest trial of their lives, they determined through God's grace to be obedient to His commands.

When a world leader made a decree to establish counterfeit worship and added the penalty of death for all who would not comply, God's people faced their time of trouble with a resolute commitment to Him. That's the model for the final days of earth's history. Then, too, God will have a group of people who are faithful to Him in the face of the antichrist's demands that everyone disobey the God of the universe. What's important in the final conflict is that we keep Jesus on center stage. We must keep Him there now. And we must keep Him there in the time of the end.

Many Christians have built up all kinds of scenarios around the idea that the antichrist will invade Jerusalem. They suggest the antichrist will create a powerful alliance in Jerusalem that Jesus will disrupt when He comes.

Well, the antichrist will be a powerful force, no doubt. But let's just remember who is invading whom. Remember that it is Jesus who is the Creator. And it is Jesus who is the Redeemer. He purchased every individual on this planet with His own blood. So the antichrist is just a temporary interruption. It's God's domain that he's invading, and he'll quickly be swept into oblivion.

Jesus is going to triumph. Keep Him on center stage.

Focus on God's Word

Now, let's look at another element of surviving the Tribulation. We must beware of any powerful so-called religious leader who draws people away from the teachings of God's Word and from obedience to God's law. The prophet Isaiah stated it succinctly to God's chosen people in his day: "To the law and to the testimony! If they do not speak according to this word, it is because there is no light in them" (Isaiah 8:20).

The prefix *anti* can mean not only "against" but also "rivaling." The antichrist is a counterfeit Jesus clothed in religious garments, who opposes the genuine Jesus by impersonating Him. That's important, because it tells us that the essence of the antichrist is deception. The movement he develops on this earth aims at deceiving and then destroying God's true people. He is pictured in Revelation 12 as the serpent who deceives as well as the dragon who destroys (Revelation 12:9). He "opposes and exalts himself above all that is called God or that is worshiped, so that he sits as God in the temple of God, showing himself that he is God" (2 Thessalonians 2:4). The antichrist usurps God's authority, establishes counterfeit worship, and places human tradition above God's commands.

In the coming time of trouble, enormous pressure will be placed upon God's people. The temptation to compromise will be enormous. If we compromise now, we'll be weakened so that it will be even easier for us to compromise then. If we cling to tradition rather than to God's Word today, selling out then will be easier. Our only safety, then, is faithfulness to God now.

Sometimes we may think we're clinging to the truth, but we're actually just clinging to tradition. Speaking of the religious leaders of His day, Jesus declared, "In vain they worship Me, teaching as doctrines the commandments of men" (Matthew 15:9). Sometimes we're tempted to cling to teachings held by a popular religious leader or by a denomination that's been our spiritual home since our youth, despite the fact that those teachings contradict Scripture. When we do that, we increase the likelihood that we'll be deceived by the antichrist.

Sometimes we think we're committed to a church when we're just committed to a familiar place, a tradition, something that feels comfortable. The more superficial our commitment to God, the more fiercely we're likely to cling to those comfortable traditions. Make sure you're standing on principles—principles clearly stated in God's Word. That will make you resilient in any time of trouble. That will keep you clinging to what is firm and immovable when everything else in this world is falling apart.

One unforgettable day, Yasser Arafat and Yitzhak Rabin stood on the lawn of the White House and extended their hands to each other. They'd cemented a historic peace agreement, taking a significant step toward ending violence in the Middle East. Arafat's people and Rabin's people had been fighting over the place for a long time. It's an important place, to be sure—Jerusalem, that ancient holy site. Israelis have a claim on it. Palestinians have a claim on it. And no one wants to give an inch. But on that occasion at the White House, those two men managed to rise above the defending of their turf. They managed to make a stand for principle.

Yasser Arafat spoke of his great hope. "Today," he said, "marks the beginning of the end of a chapter of pain and suffering which has lasted throughout this century. My people are hoping that this agreement which we are signing today will usher in an age of peace."[1]

Yitzhak Rabin also waxed eloquent. He said, "We who have come from a land where parents bury their children, we who have fought against you, the Palestinians, we say to you today in a loud and a clear voice: enough of blood and tears. Enough!"[2]

Enough of bloodshed. Enough of suffering. Enough of tears. Enough of hatred that's passed from one generation to the next. That's a principle worth standing on. And, at least for a few minutes, peace prevailed. There was a pause in Jerusalem's long tribulation.

We can make it through the time of trouble. We can make it through *any* time of trouble because God has shown us how. He's shown us how to stand on principle. He's promised to write His law in our hearts and in our minds. He has promised to give us the courage to stand for the truth of His Word. That's why we can stand against the antichrist. That's why we can stand against all his deceptions. That's why we can stand strong in the end.

The antichrist will work hard to deceive us, but we don't have to be deceived. We don't have to be drawn into his movement. We can make a better choice—fixing our eyes on Jesus, "the author and perfecter of our faith." We can keep Jesus on center stage. We can join a better movement—a movement for grace, for faith, for God's holy law, for obedience. We can take a better stand—one based on principle instead of just on a place.

Don't fall for the smoothest voices. Don't just shuffle down the easiest path. Let Jesus' love compel you. Let Him move you. Let His Spirit make His principles live within you. Follow His truth wherever it may lead you. Follow it even if it leads you away from the comfortable. Follow it even if it leads you away from the familiar. Let God's principles mold your opinions. Find a fellowship where you soak in His Word. Join the race. Keep the faith. Win the prize. Make that commitment now in the name of Jesus.

Endnotes

[1] White House Office of the Press Secretary, "Remarks at the Signing of the Israeli-Palestinian Declaration of Principles, Washington, D.C., 13 September 1993," *Journal of Palestine Studies* 23, no. 2 (Winter 1994): 119–124, http://www.palestine-studies.org/files/pdf/jps/5330.pdf.

[2] Ibid.

Chapter 10

Eternal Security

If you could have your own personal heaven on earth, what would it be like? What pictures come to your mind when you imagine an ideal place, an ideal environment? All of us nurture some dream deep inside, something that embodies our secret longings.

The Palestinian farmer in Gaza, trying to nudge a bit of wheat out of the stubborn soil, has a dream. It's a dream that keeps him going through hard times and through endless conflicts. He dreams of a free Palestinian state—a true, sovereign homeland where he can put down roots and watch his grandchildren grow up, proud of their identity.

The Israeli businessman relocating to Tel Aviv has a dream. It's a dream that has motivated him to move his home and business in his middle age. He wants to launch a computer company. He dreams that it will bring financial success and prosperity. He also dreams of a secure nation of Israel, with borders clearly established. He dreams of a Jewish homeland safe from terrorism, where he can watch his grandchildren grow up in peace.

These are the dreams that keep countless people going in the Middle East, dreams that keep them hoping, dreams that keep them struggling. But fulfilling those dreams is another matter. The problem is that the two peoples have different dreams for the same place. That's particularly true of Jerusalem. Take away the city, and you take away the foundational dream of both the Palestinians and the Israelis. That's why there are so many showdowns in this place, so many confrontations. Nobody wants to give up their dreams. That would be like losing their identity, giving up on who they really are.

Our dreams—our hopes for the future—often determine the nature of our struggles and the shape of our lives. We can't stop those longings. It's part of what makes us human.

Does that mean that we're doomed to frustration? Does it mean that all dreams are dangerous—that there's no hope of ever resolving conflicts like those in Jerusalem? There is a better dream, a different slant on the future. It's a dream that I believe enables us to live with much more hope and a lot less frustration.

Let's look at this wonderful dream. It's the big one. It's the dream that has seeded many other dreams. This dream comes to us from the Bible.

In the previous chapter, we considered why the second coming of Jesus really is the end of history—why, according to the Bible, human destinies are decided at that point. In this chapter, we're going to focus on a thousand-year period in Revelation 20 known as the millennium. The word *millennium* isn't in the Bible. It comes from Latin: *mille,* which means "one thousand," and *-ennium,* which means "a period of years." Jesus' return ends the current age and begins the millennium—a thousand years of peace under Jesus' rule. Christians around the world dream of that time and impatiently look forward to the day when that dream becomes reality. It's important that we understand the nature of this great hope and what it is based on.

Only a few Bible passages mention the millennium. Unfortunately, the popular picture of what it's going to be like—which has become prevalent in North American Evangelicalism in recent years—is based on a mistaken interpretation of the Bible.

The city of Jerusalem is a central element of this view of the millennium. When Jesus returns, it is said, He will set up a kingdom on earth, headquartered in Jerusalem. Israel will prosper. Jerusalem will become a glorious place. Believers will rule with Jesus and become involved in the judgment.

A temple will be built in Jerusalem, and animals will be sacrificed there, memorializing what Jesus accomplished on the cross.

Believers will be sent out to all nations as missionaries, and entire nations will be converted.

Those who hold this view of what will happen during the millennium base it on Old Testament prophecies about the nation of Israel—about the future of Israel.

The beginning of the millennium

Let's look at a few things that, based on what Scripture tells us, we can say for sure about the millennium. We'll start with two facts about the beginning of this thousand-year period.

Revelation 19 pictures the Second Coming. John writes, "I saw heaven opened, and behold, a white horse. And He who sat on him was called Faithful and True. . . . And the armies in heaven, clothed in fine linen, white and clean, followed Him on white horses" (Revelation 19:11, 14).

So, Jesus comes to earth as King of kings. Heaven invades human history. And something wonderful happens as a result—the faithful believers who died before Jesus' return are restored to life. This resurrection at the Second Coming marks the beginning of the millennium. John the revelator wrote, "Blessed and holy is he who has part in the first resurrection. Over such the second death has no power, but they shall be priests of God and of Jesus, and shall reign with Him a thousand years" (Revelation 20:6). Those who are raised to life in this resurrection—the "first resurrection"—will live and reign with Jesus for a thousand years—in other words, for a millennium.

In 1 Thessalonians, Paul gives us a striking picture of Jesus' second coming. He says,

> The Lord Himself will descend from heaven with a shout, with the voice of an archangel, and with the trumpet of God. And the dead in Christ will rise first. Then we who are alive and remain shall be caught up together with them in the clouds to meet the Lord in the air. And thus we shall

always be with the Lord (1 Thessalonians 4:16, 17).

The righteous living, together with the righteous dead, who have been resurrected, rise up into the clouds to meet the Lord in the air, and from this point on they will "always be with the Lord"! So, during the millennium, there are no righteous people on earth—dead or alive!

Here's another interesting point. The believers are pictured as being inside that city—inside the New Jerusalem: "The city had no need of the sun or of the moon to shine in it, for the glory of God illuminated it. The Lamb is its light. And the nations of those who are saved shall walk in its light" (Revelation 21:23, 24). The Lamb of God is a glorious light illuminating that city, and all those who are saved, those who follow the Lamb, walk in that light.

What about the wicked? Do they continue to live on earth when Jesus has come and taken the righteous to live with Him?

The prophet Jeremiah gives us quite a detailed description of conditions on earth after the Second Coming. He says,

> I beheld the earth, and indeed it was without form, and void; and the heavens, they had no light. I beheld the mountains, and indeed they trembled, and all the hills moved back and forth. I beheld, and indeed there was no man, and all the birds of the heaven had fled. I beheld, and indeed the fruitful land was a wilderness, and all its cities were broken down at the presence of the LORD, by His fierce anger (Jeremiah 4:23–26).

There are some extremely important expressions in this passage. Jeremiah declared that the earth is "without form, and void." Moses used the same words in Genesis 1:2 to describe what the earth was like before God created dry land and plants and animals. But Jeremiah certainly wasn't talking about Creation week. He speaks about the birds of heaven as fleeing, and what had been fruitful land becoming a wilderness, and cities being broken down. These things didn't exist on earth when God began to create it. And it's the presence of the Lord and His fierce anger that has caused all this. The event that the prophet was describing is the return of our Lord.

Jeremiah then adds that there was "no man" and explains, "At that day the slain of the LORD shall be from one end of the earth even to the other end of the earth. They shall not be lamented, or gathered, or buried" (Jeremiah 25:33). So, at Jesus' second coming, He draws to Himself those who are righteous in Him, while the wicked try to hide themselves. But sinners cannot live in the presence of the holy God, and so they die.

Here then are the two facts about the beginning of the millennium that we should keep in mind: (1) the righteous dead, resurrected at the Second Coming, and the righteous living rise from earth to be with Jesus where He is, and (2) the wicked are slain by the brightness of His coming.

So, no people live on earth during the millennium. They're all gone—either dead or living with Christ in heaven. Satan and his angels are imprisoned here—restricted to this desolate earth and bound in the sense that there's nothing for them to do here—there's no one here to tempt (Revelation 20:1–3). Satan now sees the tragic result of his rebellion against God. The words "the wages of sin is death" (Romans 6:23) echo and re-echo throughout the universe. God is the Source of life, and when people choose to separate themselves from Him, they're choosing to separate themselves from life. They're choosing to die. Death is the ultimate fate of those who reject God.

The millennium's end

Now let's look at two facts about the end of the millennium. Revelation 20:6 speaks of a "first resurrection." That implies there's a second resurrection too. Who is raised in that resurrection, and when does it take place?

Jesus told His disciples about the second resurrection. He said, "The hour is coming in which all who are in their graves shall hear His voice and come forth—those who have done good to the resurrection of life, and those who have done evil to the resurrection of condemnation" (John 5:28, 29). Obviously, the people who are brought to life in an event called the "resurrection of condemnation" aren't the saints. They aren't believers. They aren't the saved.

The author of Revelation also pictures two resurrections. After he writes about the resurrection of the "blessed and holy," he turns to "the rest of the dead"—the people who have rejected God. He says that they "did not live again *until . . .*" (Revelation 20:5; emphasis added). So, they *do* eventually live again. They are raised from death to life, but they return to life in the second resurrection, the "resurrection of condemnation."

Revelation 20:5 also answers our question about when the second resurrection takes place. It says, "The rest of the dead did not live again *until the thousand years were finished*" (emphasis added). So here are the two facts about the end of the millennium that will keep us from misunderstanding what it involves: (1) there will be a second resurrection in which the wicked will be brought back to life; and (2) the second resurrection takes place at the end of the millennium.

During the millennium, then, the wicked are dead. Lifeless. Gone. They aren't resurrected till the end of the thousand years. That means that during the millennium, there's no one on earth for believers to evangelize. Nobody's out there waiting to hear the good news. What, then, would be the point of declaring the earthly Jerusalem to be the center of Jesus' kingdom and saying that God's light is shining from that city to all nations? What purpose would they serve when there are no living human beings on the earth?

In verses 2 and 3 of Revelation 21, we read what happens after Jesus' thousand-year reign of peace:

Then I, John, saw the holy city, New Jerusalem, coming

down out of heaven from God, prepared as a bride adorned for her husband. And I heard a loud voice from heaven saying, "Behold, the tabernacle of God is with men, and He will dwell with them."

At the beginning of the millennium, a glorious Jesus comes from heaven down to earth. At the end of the millennium, a glorious city, the New Jerusalem, comes from heaven down to earth. Notice what the "loud voice from heaven" says—"The tabernacle of God is with men, and He will dwell with them." If, as the popular belief has it, Jesus has spent the past thousand years ruling earth from Jerusalem, why does Revelation tell us here that God has come to earth to dwell here with human beings? An interesting question.

Let's review what we've found. At the beginning of the millennium, those who have rejected God die, and believers rise up into the clouds to meet Jesus and to "always be with" Him. At the end of the millennium, the New Jerusalem comes down from heaven and the believers are inside that city. How do we best put all these facts together? I believe they also point to the conclusion that believers spend the millennium in heaven. They don't reign with Jesus on the earth; they reign with Him in heaven.

The second coming of Jesus ends our history on the unregenerated earth and begins our sojourn in heaven. What Jesus Himself promised goes to the heart of the Christian dream:

> "In My Father's house are many mansions; if it were not so, I would have told you. I go to prepare a place for you. And if I go and prepare a place for you, I will come again and receive you to Myself; that where I am, there you may be also" (John 14:2, 3).

Where did Jesus go after His resurrection?
To heaven.

Where is His Father's house?

In heaven.

Where is Jesus preparing a place for us?

In heaven.

Where does He want to take us so we can be with Him?

To heaven.

So, believers spend the millennium in heaven. The apostle John leaves no doubt about where we will be and what we will be doing during that time. God gave him a view of heaven, and he testifies about what he saw:

> I saw thrones, and they sat on them, and judgment was committed to them.... Blessed and holy is he who has part in the first resurrection. Over such the second death has no power, but they shall be priests of God and of Jesus and shall reign with Him a thousand years (Revelation 20:4, 6).

We will reign with Jesus in heaven for a thousand years. We will act as judges there, having been given the privilege of reviewing the cases of the wicked.

During those thousand years, God will enhance the security of the universe by answering all of our questions about His fairness. He will help us understand more fully how much He loves us and the horrendous consequences of sin. We will experience the love and peace and joy He offers us in a way we never could before. And we will see more clearly that He has done everything possible to save every human being and that those who are lost suffer that fate because of their own selfish choices.

At the end of the millennium, believers return to earth in the New Jerusalem. Then the wicked experience the second resurrection—the resurrection of condemnation. They stand before God's throne and see one last panoramic vision of their lives. They realize that God has done everything possible to save them—that He could have done no more.

Revelation tells us that then Satan "will go out to deceive the nations . . . to gather them together to battle. . . . They went up on the breadth of the earth and surrounded the camp of the saints and the beloved city" (verses 8, 9). The wicked try to attack the Holy City, and at that point God executes judgment against them. "Fire [comes] down from God out of heaven and [devours] them" (verse 9).

The wicked aren't lost because they didn't have the opportunity to be saved, but because they rejected the opportunities God graciously gave them. They aren't lost because God didn't love them and didn't want them saved, but because they spurned that love and rejected His offer.

At this point, every being in the universe will kneel before God's throne, and every tongue will confess that Jesus is Lord (Philippians 2:9–11; Revelation 20:11–13). Then God will create a new heaven and a new earth, and the New Jerusalem, which is His home and has become our home, settles down upon this renewed planet for eternity (2 Peter 3:13; Revelation 21:1).

Why it matters

Why is understanding the Bible truth about the millennium important? Why does it matter? After all, Jesus' reign is going to be a good thing. It would be a good thing wherever it happened. The most important element of its goodness is that Jesus is ruling, whether from earth or heaven. However, a millennium centered in heaven offers us a more attractive hope, a better dream while we are here.

First, a true understanding—a biblical understanding—of the millennium establishes forever our belief in God's fairness and justice. During those thousand years, we'll see that God has done everything He could to save every person who has ever lived on planet Earth. When the great controversy between good and evil is finally settled, the universe will be secure forever. Sin will never raise its ugly head again. God's love will be indelibly written in the hearts and minds of His people.

Second, people's dreams of an earthly millennium are easily exploited. Many cult leaders and fanatics have used them. Adolf Hitler used such dreams in his attempt to establish a Third Reich that would last a thousand years. Revelation tells us that in the future, the antichrist will exploit the same human longings. Revelation 13 says he will perform great signs—miracles, really—even appearing to make fire come down from heaven. He exercises great authority. He speaks great blasphemies. He controls every tribe, tongue, and nation. It will seem that the whole world is following him. People will even worship him, saying, "Who is able to make war with him?"

What enables the antichrist to get such a hold on people's imaginations? Why is he able to control them so completely? Why do so many fall for his deceptions?

People will fall for him for the same reason they fall for cult leaders today. These charismatic figures promise peace on earth. They promise paradise here and now. They say they're going to set up a special kingdom, and they persuade their followers to wage war on those who stand in the way of their utopia. The antichrist will do the same things.

In his letter to the Colossians, Paul gives us some great advice about how to dream. "If . . . you were raised with Christ [from spiritual death], seek those things which are above, where Christ is, sitting at the right hand of God. Set your mind on things above, not on things on the earth" (Colossians 3:1, 2). If you've been raised to a new life with Jesus, then keep looking up. Focus your attention where Jesus is. Fix your hope on the Jesus who rules at God's right hand. Those who built the Tower of Babel were trying to get themselves to heaven through their own hard work. We can't make the millennium the blessing God intends it to be for us. It's what God puts into the millennium that makes it the blessing He intends us to have.

Here's another reason why a millennium spent in heaven is better than one spent on earth: heaven has enough room for everybody. That's certainly not true of sacred places on earth, sacred places like

Jerusalem. Human nature being what it is, each attempt to establish a heavenly kingdom on earth generates turf wars. It happens over and over. There just is not enough heaven-on-earth to satisfy everyone.

What did Jesus say about the place He's preparing for us in heaven? He said there are many mansions in His Father's house. There's plenty of room. That's what heaven is all about. It's about God's wide welcome. It is about God urging more and more people to come to His great banquet table.

Here's an interesting detail about the New Jerusalem: "The city is laid out as a square; its length is as great as its breadth. And he measured the city with the reed: twelve thousand furlongs. Its length, breadth, and height are equal" (Revelation 21:16).

Twelve thousand furlongs amounts to about fifteen hundred miles. If we take these measurements literally, we have this incredible cube more than a thousand miles long and wide and high. What is the point here? Simply this: that there's plenty of room in God's glorious city—plenty of room for everyone. Heaven is not a zero-sum game. It has the length and breadth and depth of Jesus' infinite love. That is better than any earthly hope. It is a hope that can widen our hearts rather than increase our conflicts.

Here's my final reason why spending the millennium in heaven is a better dream. In heaven, we all stand on exactly the same ground. We're all immigrants there.

In 1993, negotiators were trying to get the Oslo peace talks between Israel and the Palestinians underway. Abu Ala was there to represent the Palestine Liberation Organization, and Uri Savir represented Israel.

The two men tested each other for a bit. Mr. Ala wondered why Israel, with its vastly superior war machine, felt so threatened by its Arabic neighbors. Mr. Savir pointed out that the Arab world had for a long time been committed to Israel's destruction. Then Mr. Ala asked his counterpart, "Where are you from?"

"Jerusalem," the Israeli replied.

"So am I," Mr. Ala said. Then he took the question back a generation. He asked, "Where is your father from?"

Mr. Savir admitted that his father was born in Europe, which Mr. Ala quickly topped by interjecting, "Mine was born in Jerusalem and still lives there."

However, Mr. Savir was not to be outdone. He challenged Mr. Ala with the question, "Why don't you ask about my grandfathers and their forebears? We could go back to King David."[1]

The real issue these men were debating was which group of people had the greater right to occupy Jerusalem. Who had the right to raise their flag above those ancient stones? That's why they were hashing over the question of who got there first. The Palestinians could claim that their ancestors had occupied the land long before the modern nation of Israel was born, while the Israelis could assert that Jews had staked a claim to Jerusalem long before that, in the days of King David.

Who got there first? Who has first claim on the sacred city? Those are the issues that people debate endlessly when staking a claim to heaven on earth.

A new and different kingdom

Jesus' heavenly millennium is a different story. It's built on different principles. Everyone stands on the same ground. We all belong because through Jesus Christ we are all members of the royal family of heaven. No one can claim he or she is more deserving of a place in paradise than is anyone else.

Do you know what's on the foundation stones of the New Jerusalem? Revelation 21:14 tells us those stones bear the names of the twelve apostles. I find that very interesting. John's name is there— John, the Son of Thunder; the man with quite a temper. And Peter's name is there—Peter, the man who habitually said the wrong thing at the wrong time. And so is the name of Thomas, the man who had such a hard time believing Jesus' promises and prophecies.

Amazingly, the foundation stones of the New Jerusalem bear the names of weak human beings! What is this telling us?

It's telling us that through faith in Jesus, we may all overcome our weaknesses and be welcomed into that glorious city. We may all find a home there. This is an assurance God gives to each of us.

But that's not all. Jesus has also placed names on all twelve of the gates in the walls of the New Jerusalem.

What names?

The names of the twelve tribes of Israel. The names of the sons of Jacob.

Who were they?

Joseph's brothers: Reuben, Simeon, Judah, and all the rest.

Think of the terrible things they did to Joseph. Think of their years of sorrow and regret. But they found their way back to the God of heaven. These names on the gates of the New Jerusalem tell us that those gates swing wide open for people who have made terrible mistakes, people who have fallen badly. If they've asked forgiveness and put themselves in God's hands, they'll find a welcome there. This is another assurance God gives to each of us.

There's still more! In ancient times, most cities had just one gate. That made it easier to keep the unwanted out. But the New Jerusalem's four great walls, which face north, south, east, and west, each have three gates. The number *three* is often used as a symbol of the Trinity. What is God saying? He's saying, "Everyone from the north—the Father, Son, and Holy Spirit say you can come in. Everyone from the south—the Father, Son, and Holy Spirit say you can come in. Everyone from the east—the Father, Son, and Holy Spirit say you can come in. Everyone from the west—the Father, Son, and Holy Spirit say you can come in."

Yes, there's plenty of good room in the New Jerusalem. We all get into that city by grace alone. We all enter through those gates into the glorious city solely because of the Father's mercy. We are accepted there because the righteousness of the beloved Son is accepted there. That's the sole reason we're allowed to enter. No other claims are accepted. No other credentials count.

Where is your hope today? What are your deepest longings attached to? Isn't it time you began looking at the unshakable things in heaven above? Isn't it time you began focusing on the risen Jesus who is preparing a place for us?

We need a bigger dream today. We need to dream of better things. We need a wider vision. We need to live our lives in the length and breadth and depth of the love of Jesus. We need to look forward to His millennium of peace. And we need to let it begin in our hearts today.

You can make God's great dream your own. As we come to the end of our journey together through the chapters of this book, would you like to make a personal commitment to Jesus Christ? Would you like to respond to the matchless charms of His love and the claims of His grace? Would you like to surrender whatever may be preventing you from being ready for His return?

If you would like to commit or to recommit your life to Jesus, I invite you to join me in praying this simple prayer:

> Dear Lord,
> Thank You, dear Lord, that You have not left us alone on this planet. Keep me from being so entangled in the things of this world that I forget the real purpose of life. Fill my heart now and forever with the hope of Your return. In Jesus' name. Amen.

Endnote

[1] Uri Savir, *The Process: 1,100 Days That Changed the Middle East* (New York: Vintage, 1998), 14, 15.

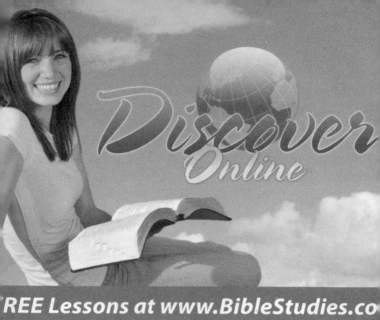

FREE Lessons at www.BibleStudies.co

It's easy to learn more about the Bible!

Call:
1-888-456-7933

Write:
Discover
P.O. Box 53055
Los Angeles, CA 90053